THE **ULTIMATE BOOK** OF
RANDOMLY
AWESOME
FACTS

I'm not from Guinea,
and I'm not a pig.

▶▶ see page 24 for more animals with the wrong names

SCHOLASTIC

THE ULTIMATE BOOK OF
RANDOMLY
AWESOME
FACTS

By Penelope Arlon,
Tory Gordon-Harris, and Karen Hood

Quizzes written by Laaren Brown

Copyright © 2015 by Scholastic Inc.

ISBN 978-0-545-82626-6

10 9 8 7 6 5 4 3 2 1   15 16 17 18 19

Printed in the U.S.A.   08
First printing, August 2015

Scholastic is constantly working to lessen the
environmental impact of our manufacturing processes.
To view our industry-leading paper procurement policy,
visit www.scholastic.com/paperpolicy.

Contents

6 The natural world

8 Eyes	24 Animals	38 Superbugs
10 Speed	26 What	40 Plants
12 Parasites	prehistoric	42 What volcanic
14 What	beast are you?	eruption
endangered	28 Dinosaurs	are you?
animal are you?	30 Ancient	44 Earth
16 Pets	animals	46 Weather
18 Senses	32 Extinction	48 Rain
20 Ouch!	34 Ocean	
22 Extreme animals	36 Rainforest	

50 SCIENCE & TECH

52 SPACE
54 MOON
56 WHAT ELEMENT OF THE PERIODIC TABLE ARE YOU?
58 SPACE TECHNOLOGY
60 LIVING IN SPACE
62 END OF THE WORLD
64 SCIENTISTS
66 PHYSICS
68 ELEMENTS
70 INVENTIONS
72 WHAT WORLD-CHANGING INVENTION ARE YOU?
74 VEHICLES
76 ROBOTS
78 CYBORGS
80 BUILDINGS
82 WHAT FAMOUS SCIENTIST ARE YOU?
84 NUMBERS
86 COMPUTERS

88 Everyday Life

90 Human body
92 Bodies
94 Sight
96 Language
98 Food
100 Where should you live?
102 More food
104 Potato chips
106 Money
108 What job is right for you?
110 Jobs
112 Explorers

114 Extreme survivors
116 States
118 Places
120 Cities
122 Sports
124 Balls
126 Movies
128 Superheroes
130 How long would you survive?
132 Music
134 Toys
136 Superstructures

138 Quiz answers
142 Index

The natural

world

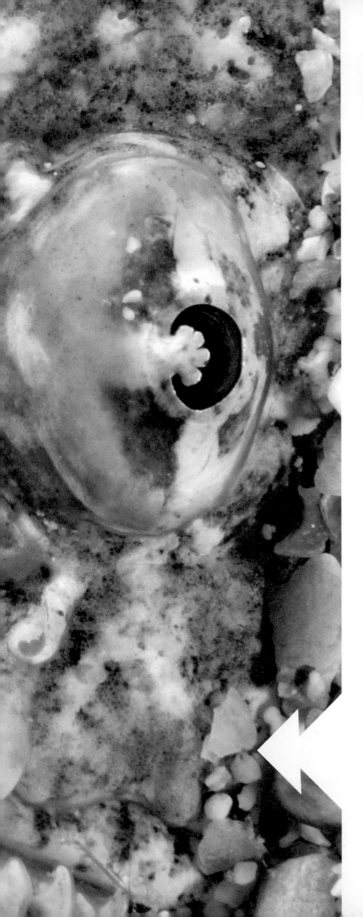

9 I spy with my creepy eyes ...

1. Mantis shrimp
This 1-foot shrimp has better eyesight than any other animal.

2. Giant squid
Most animals' eyes are smaller than oranges. A giant squid's eye is as big as your head.

3. Dragonfly
Dragonflies section off what they see in a grid. They move around to keep prey in the same section, then grab it.

4. Goat
Goats have rectangular pupils. This means that they can see a panoramic 320 to 340 degrees. So they can almost see behind themselves.

5. Stargazer
This fish buries itself in sand, eyes staring up. When prey passes by, it throws 50 killer volts of electricity from its eyes to stun the prey.

6. Reindeer
As the days grow darker in winter, reindeer eyes change colors from gold to blue. Creepy, Rudolph!

7. Scallop
Yuck—scallops have 100 eyes around their shells. Remember that the next time you eat some!

8. Tarsier
A tarsier's eyes are each as big as its brain. These enormous eyes make the tarsier an epic hunter—useful, since tarsiers refuse to eat vegetables.

9. Ogre-faced spider
This spider will see you before you see it. It has the best eyesight in the spider world—using all 8 of its eyes.

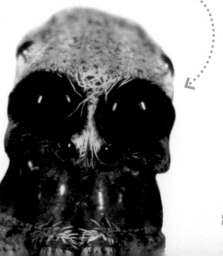

10 animals that can sprint faster than Usain Bolt

2. Pronghorn (55 mph)

3. Horse (55 mph)

4. Lion (50 mph)

1. Cheetah (65 mph)

5. Brown hare (45 mph)

10 ocean swimmers that can

9. Gentoo penguin (22 mph)

7. Salmon (28 mph)

Michael Phelps (4.7 mph)

10. Cod (5 mph)

8. Common octopus (25 mph)

8 SUPERFAST SPEED FACTS

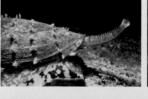

1st 2nd 3rd

CHOMP!

1. Fastest bite
The trap-jaw ant can bite at 145 mph.

2. Fastest poison
The cone snail's poison kills instantly.

3. Fastest tongue
The palm salamander shoots out its tongue at 150 mph!

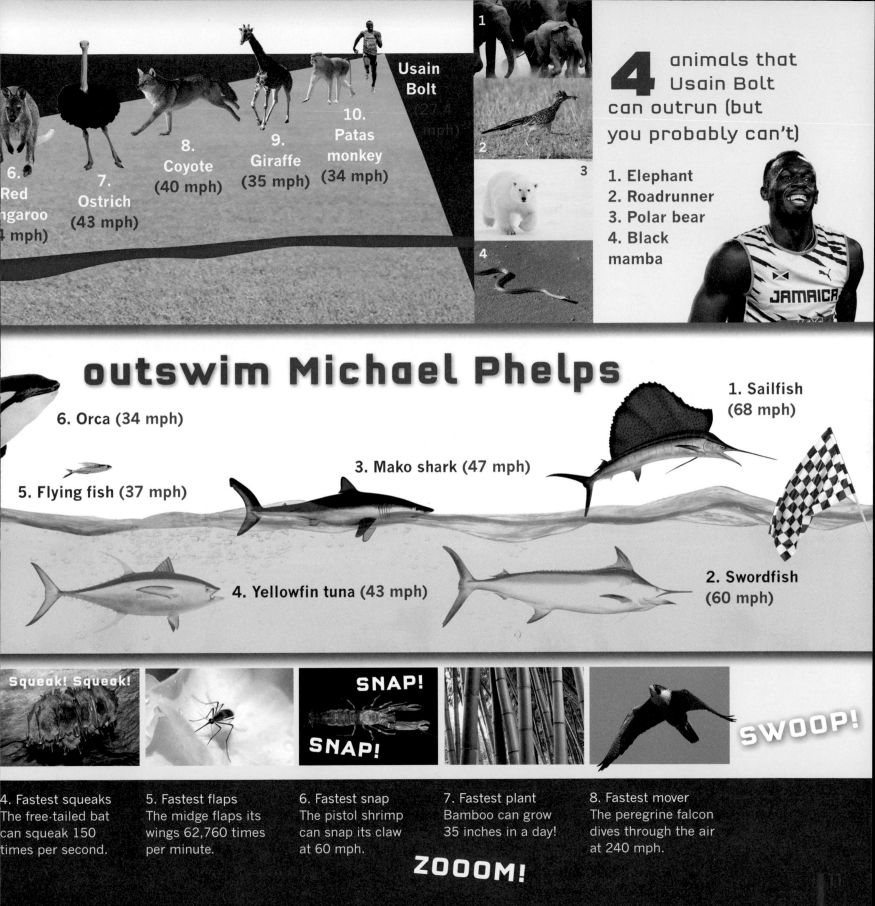

4 animals that Usain Bolt can outrun (but you probably can't)

1. Elephant
2. Roadrunner
3. Polar bear
4. Black mamba

Usain Bolt

6. Red kangaroo (44 mph)

7. Ostrich (43 mph)

8. Coyote (40 mph)

9. Giraffe (35 mph)

10. Patas monkey (34 mph)

outswim Michael Phelps

1. Sailfish (68 mph)

6. Orca (34 mph)

5. Flying fish (37 mph)

3. Mako shark (47 mph)

4. Yellowfin tuna (43 mph)

2. Swordfish (60 mph)

Squeak! Squeak!

SNAP! SNAP!

SWOOP!

4. Fastest squeaks
The free-tailed bat can squeak 150 times per second.

5. Fastest flaps
The midge flaps its wings 62,760 times per minute.

6. Fastest snap
The pistol shrimp can snap its claw at 60 mph.

7. Fastest plant
Bamboo can grow 35 inches in a day!

8. Fastest mover
The peregrine falcon dives through the air at 240 mph.

ZOOOM!

8 BLOOD-SUCKING BUGS . . .

Bedbugs

. . . THAT BITE YOU AND LEAVE YOU WITH A DISEASE, A RASH, OR AN ITCHY BUMP

Tick

1. Bedbug
2. Mosquito
3. Flea
4. Tick
5. Leech
6. Human botfly
7. Scab mite
8. Tsetse fly

Mosquito

7 parasites that TAKE CONTROL of their hosts

1. **Brine shrimp tapeworm**
The larva of this tapeworm takes over a brine shrimp's brain, turning the shrimp red and making it swim in groups. This makes it more likely to be eaten by a flamingo.

2. **Horsehair worm**
The larva of this worm takes over a cricket's brain and makes it leap into water. The now-grown worm wriggles free as the cricket drowns!

3. **Tongue-eating isopod**
This parasite eats a fish's tongue—and then becomes the tongue! It feeds on the food that the fish catches.

4. **Zombie fungus**
This fungus invades carpenter ants. It bursts out of the ants' heads, then infects other ants in the colony.

5. Emerald cockroach wasp
This wasp injects chemicals into a cockroach's brain. It steers the roach by the antennae, like they're reins! Then the wasp lays its eggs on the roach. The eggs hatch, and the larvae eat the roach alive. Gross!

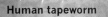

Human tapeworm

6. Ladybug parasite
This wasp lays its egg in a ladybug's belly. The larva takes over the ladybug's brain. The ladybug— the perfect zombie bodyguard— protects the larva until it becomes an adult!

7. Human tapeworm
Tapeworms 30 feet long have been found living in human intestines.

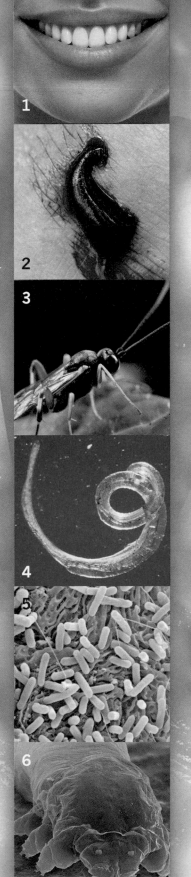

1

2

3

4

5

6

6
parasites you should learn to love!

1. Good bacteria zap tooth decay in your mouth.

2. Bloodsucking leeches can clear infections.

3. Parasitic wasps can help get rid of farm pests.

4. Some worms that live in human intestines can cure allergies.

5. Other friendly bacteria, in your stomach, wage war on diseases and keep you healthy.

6. *Demodex* mites sometimes live in your eyelashes—and you don't even know it!

What ENDANGERED

The world is full of cool animals. But too many are in danger of dying out. If you were an endangered animal, what would you be?

1. How do you like to get around?

A Bus. You can see the whole town and get to school.

B Airplane. It means vacation! Or a visit to Aunt Martha . . .

C Bike. You can go anywhere. You feel so *freeee*!

D Sedan chair. Your carriers will take you wherever you want to go.

2. What famous landmark would you love to see?

A The Taj Mahal in India.

B The Great Wall of China.

C Machu Picchu in Peru.

D The pyramids in Egypt.

3. What do you like to do in your spare time?

A Hang out with friends.

B Relax with a good book.

C Make something crafty.

D Watch TV.

ANIMAL are you?

4. When you have a problem, you . . .

A Use logic and reason to solve it.

B Use charm to talk your way out of it.

C Are not surprised. You're always in trouble!

D Don't stress about it. Everything will work out for the best.

5. What characteristic do you value most in a friend?

A Strength.

B Smarts.

C Silliness.

D Sincerity.

6. In science class, you have to throw an egg off a roof without breaking it. What do you do?

A Wrap the egg in lots of padding and put it in a sturdy box, then in another box. Can't be too careful!

B Draw an elaborate face on the egg and give it a name. Get very attached to your egg.

C Leave most of the work to your teammates. They seem to know what they're doing!

D Construct a harness and parachute for the egg, then hope for the best. On to other projects!

7. You have birthday money. What will you buy?

A A fuzzy coat.

B A bouquet of flowers.

C Something to play with—maybe a game or a toy.

D A dozen of the best chocolate chip cookies ever.

Panda? Macaw? Turn to page 138 to add up your score and find out what endangered animal you are!

6 famous PETS

1. **Christian the lion cub** was bought at Harrods, a London department store, in 1969.

2. **A dormouse named Xarifa** was owned by author Beatrix Potter and featured in one of her books.

4. **Spike,** cartoonist Charles Schulz's dog, was the inspiration for Snoopy.

5. **A one-legged rooster** lived in the White House when Theodore Roosevelt was US president.

4 priciest pets

1. In 2006, a foal called the Green Monkey sold for $16 million.

2. In 2014, a Tibetan mastiff sold for $2 million in China.

3. In 2008, Sir Lancelot, a Labrador, was cloned for $155,000 after he died.

4. In 2014, Paris Hilton bought the smallest Pomeranian ever for $13,000.

3. Congo the chimp produced about 400 paintings! Pablo Picasso owned one.

6. Paul the octopus correctly predicted the winners of World Cup soccer games in 2010!

5 BRILLIANTLY BRAVE BEASTS

1. Gustav the pigeon carried the first news of D-Day in World War II.

2. Unsinkable Sam, a German cat, survived 3 shipwrecks during WWII.

3. Jet the Alsatian rescued 150 Londoners trapped under rubble in WWII.

4. Upstart the horse controlled traffic following a bomb in London in 1947.

5. Salty and Roselle, Labrador guide dogs, led their visually impaired owners out of the World Trade Center on 9/11.

Cat and dog record breakers

1. **Largest cat:** Maine coon
2. **Biggest litter:** 19 kittens (to a Burmese-Siamese cat)
3. **Least hairy breed:** Sphynx
4. **Loudest purr:** A gray tabby named Smokey is as loud as a hair dryer!

1. **Largest dog:** Great Dane
2. **Smallest dog:** Chihuahua
3. **Biggest litter:** 24 pups (to a Neapolitan mastiff)
4. **Highest jumper:** A greyhound named Cinderella May jumped 68 inches!

need a haircut? 4 HAIRIEST PETS IN THE WORLD

1. **Furriest dog:** Kyra, a komondor
2. **Furriest cat:** Colonel Meow, a Himalayan-Persian mix
3. **Fluffiest bunny breed:** Angora
4. **Hairiest pig breed:** Mangalitsa

6 animal senses that will BLOW YOUR MIND

8 F-F-F-FREAKY animal senses

1. A catfish has about 100,000 taste buds all over its body—it is a swimming tongue!

2. A cricket's ears are on its knees.

3. A snake smells with its forked tongue.

4. A star-nosed mole has 22 tiny trunks that can smell and dig!

5. A rat's nostrils work independently of each other.

7 SCARY shark stories to keep you on land FOREVER

1. A shark can smell a single drop of blood in the amount of water that would fill an Olympic-size swimming pool.

2. A shark can tell exactly which direction a scent is coming from.

1. Built-in GPS
A pigeon can find its way by sensing Earth's magnetic field, just like a compass does.

2. Heat sensor
A vampire bat can sense the heat of your blood running through your veins—creepy!

Vampire bat

3. Weather forecasting
Elephants can feel thunderstorms 100 miles away.

4. Fire alarm
Jewel beetles can sense forest fires from 50 miles away.

5. Echolocation
A dolphin makes a sound and listens to how it echoes to estimate distances.

6. Electricity
A duck-billed platypus can sense electrical charges in fish.

6. A Gardiner's Seychelles frog has no ears. It "hears" other frogs through its mouth, which acts like an echo chamber.

7. A crocodile's face is more sensitive than human fingertips.

8. A blowfly tastes with 3,000 sensory hairs on its feet.

3. A shark can see as well as a cat can in dim light.

4. A shark can hear the sound of a wounded animal from over a mile away.

5. A shark can sense an animal buried in the sand by the electricity it gives off.

6. A shark can sense vibrations from the thrashings of an injured fish.

7. A shark "taste checks" each piece of prey to find out if it is poisonous.

HEY-WE'RE-AMAZING-TOO

10

HUMAN SENSES

1. Sight
2. Touch
3. Smell
4. Taste
5. Hearing
6. Pain
7. Balance
8. Itching
9. Temperature
10. Kinesthesia (awareness of body movements)

10 OUCH!

piercing insect stings, as tested and described by entomologist Justin Schmidt

10. Sweat bee
A tiny spark has singed a single hair on your arm.

9. Fire ant
Sharp, sudden, mildly alarming. Like walking across a shag carpet and reaching for the light switch.

8. Bullhorn acacia ant
A rare, piercing, elevated sort of pain. Someone has fired a staple into your cheek.

7. Bald-faced hornet
Rich, hearty, slightly crunchy. Similar to getting your hand mashed in a revolving door.

6. Yellow jacket
Hot and smoky, almost irreverent. Imagine W. C. Fields extinguishing a cigar on your tongue.

5. Honeybee
Like a match head that flips off and burns on your skin.

4. Red harvester ant
Bold and unrelenting. Somebody is using a drill to excavate your ingrown toenail.

3. Paper wasp
Caustic and burning. Distinctly bitter aftertaste. Like spilling a beaker of hydrochloric acid on a paper cut.

2. Tarantula hawk
Blinding, fierce, shockingly electric. . . . If you get stung by one, you might as well lie down and scream.

1. Bullet ant
Pure, intense, brilliant pain. Like firewalking over flaming charcoal with a 3-inch nail in your heel.

6 EAR-SPLITTINGLY

1. **The howler monkey** is the loudest land animal.

2. **Katydids** can be as loud as chain saws or helicopters.

3. **The coqui,** a type of frog, is as loud as a lawn mower.

9 DEADLY

5 TOXIC TERRORS

1. Poison dart frog
2. Puffer fish
3. Ifrit (a type of bird)
4. Puss moth caterpillar
5. Almost every jellyfish

DON'T TOUCH!

1. Mosquito
Spreads the disease malaria, causing the highest human death toll.

2. Male African elephant
For sheer brute strength.

3. Box jellyfish
Lethal in the oceans.

4. Inland taipan (a snake)
Lethal on land.

5. Great white shark
The perfect killing machine.

LOUD animals (COVER YOUR EARS!)

4. **Oilbirds** are some of the loudest birds. Thousands squawking together in a cave are unbearable!

5. **The blue whale** is the loudest single creature in water.

6. **Pistol shrimp** snap their claws. Together, hundreds of them make the loudest noise in the ocean.

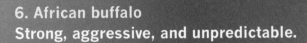

KILLERS

6. **African buffalo**
Strong, aggressive, and unpredictable.

7. *Clostridium botulinum* (a bacterium)
A mass killer—1 teaspoon could kill the entire population of the US.

8. **Siafu (an ant)**
Deadly when part of an army.

9. **Blue-ringed octopus**
Supervenomous . . . and smart.

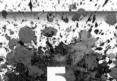

HOLD YOUR NOSE!

8 OF THE STINKIEST ANIMALS ON THE PLANET

1. Bombardier beetle
This critter squirts a foul, boiling acid from its bottom if threatened.

2. Wolverine
It sprays a supersmelly stench to mark its territory.

3. Stinkbug
Watch out! If threatened, it can spray its stink several inches.

4. Skunk
Its offensive smell can travel over a mile.

5. Fulmar chick
These baby birds can throw foul-smelling vomit at enemies 5 feet away.

6. Tasmanian devil
Don't hassle the devil! It smells when it's stressed.

7. Hoatzin
Also called a stinkbird, it smells of manure because of its lousy digestion.

8. Musk ox
It has extremely stinky pee that clings to its hairy bottom!

5 bright ideas we STOLE from animals

1. A shark's skin
Scientists have created a material like sharkskin that is made of tiny, sharp scales. The military may cover boats with it, to keep unwanted creatures from sticking to the boats.

2. The back of the Namib Desert beetle
Researchers have made a bumpy material inspired by this beetle's back. The beetle collects dew that runs down the ridges of its back to its mouth.

3. A gecko's grip
A new adhesive copies the way the tiny hairs on a gecko's feet enable it to run across ceilings.

4. A spider's web
Scientists have made medical tubes that are sticky like spiderwebs. These are gentle enough to use on babies' skin.

5. A butterfly's wing
The way a butterfly's wings shine has inspired scientists to make computer screens that can be read in bright sunlight.

6 ANIMALS

IT'S CALLED WHAT?

9 ANIMALS WITH THE WRONG NAME

1. **A whale shark** is not a whale. It's a shark.
2. **A starfish** is not a fish. It's an echinoderm.
3. **A killer whale** is not a whale. It's a dolphin.
4. **A bald eagle** is not bald. It has a cap of white feathers.
5. **A flying fox** is not a fox. It's a bat.
6. **A prairie dog** is not a dog. It's a rodent.
7. **A sea horse** is not a horse. It's a fish.
8. **An American buffalo** is not a buffalo. It's a bison.
9. **A guinea pig** is not from Guinea and is not a pig. It's a rodent from South America.

1. The olinguito is a raccoonlike mammal that was found in the Andes mountains in South America.
2. Skeleton shrimp were found in a reef cave off California.
3. The Tinkerbell fairy fly is a tiny, tiny wasp found in Costa Rica.

4. The Cape Melville leaf-tailed gecko was found in a newly discovered rainforest in Australia!
5. The domed land snail, a blind cave dweller, was found in Croatia.

6. A new type of amoeboid protists, strange creatures that mimic sponges when grouped together, were found in an underwater cave near Spain.

10 MOST COMMON ANIMAL PHOBIAS

1. Fear of spiders
2. Fear of snakes
3. Fear of wasps
4. Fear of birds
5. Fear of mice
6. Fear of fish
7. Fear of bees
8. Fear of dogs
9. Fear of caterpillars
10. Fear of cats

What PREHISTORIC

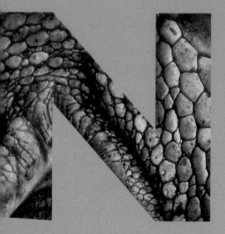

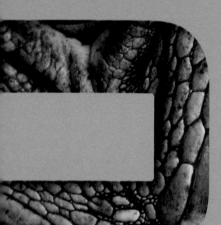

Huge animals once roamed the planet. If you traveled back in time, which mighty beast would you be? Take this quiz and find out!

1. You're sitting down to a nice dinner. What's on the plate?

A
Red meat. *Raaaar!*

B
A healthy salad.

C
Fried calamari.

D
Roadkill.

2. What would your dream vacation involve?

A
Somewhere tropical and exotic.

B
A safari in Africa, with a barbecue every evening.

C
Anywhere with plenty of fun activities.

D
Oh, you know. Just hanging out.

3. If you were a fruit, which would you be?

A

B

C

D

BEAST are you?

4. What kinds of clothes do you like to wear?

A	B	C	D
I have to be warm ALL THE TIME. And I mean ALL THE TIME.	Something skintight, with a tasteful print.	I like big, fluffy, woolly coats.	Something really funky and fashionable.

5. Which is worse, your bark or your bite?

A Definitely my bite!

B Probably my bark.

C Neither—I try to be chill.

D Both—but I usually give a warning before I attack!

6. Always in a rush? Or quiet and controlled? What's your speed?

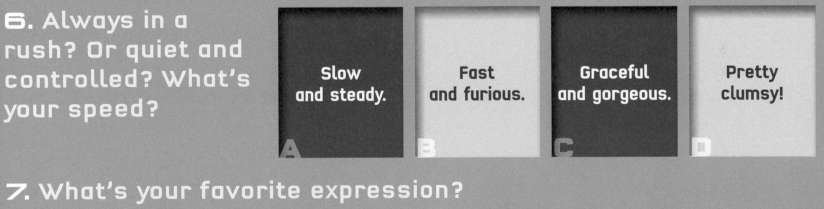

A	B	C	D
Slow and steady.	Fast and furious.	Graceful and gorgeous.	Pretty clumsy!

7. What's your favorite expression?

A	B	C	D
OMG!	YOLO!	LOL!	Zzzzzz.

Woolly mammoth? *T. rex*? Turn to page 138 to add up your score and find out what beast you are!

9

ways to die by dinosaur

1. Get thumped by *Ankylosaurus*'s clubbed tail.

2. Be torn open by a leaping *Velociraptor* with 2-inch sickle-shaped claws.

3. Have your bones crushed in *Giganotosaurus*'s massive jaws.

4. Get spiked to death by *Iguanodon*'s thumb claw.

5. Be attacked at the lakeside by a huge *Spinosaurus* shooting out of the water.

6. Be chased by a pack of 18-foot-long *Utahraptor*s.

7. Be stabbed by a giant *Triceratops* horn.

8. Have your insides ripped out by the biggest claws of all—those of *Therizinosaurus*.

9. Be outwitted by the smartest dinosaur, *Troödon*.

10. OUT-THERE, brand-new dinosaur names

1. *Rhinorex*
("king nose")

2. *Xenoceratops*
("alien-horned face")

3. *Nanuqsaurus hoglundi*
("Hoglund's polar bear lizard")

4. *Tachiraptor*
("thief of Tachira")

5. *Nasutoceratops titusi*
("Titus's big-nosed horned face")

6. *Kosmoceratops*
("ornamented horned face")

7. *Changyuraptor*
("long-feathered thief")

8. *Rukwatitan bisepultus*
("twice-buried giant from Lake Rukwa")

9. *Deinocheirus mirificus*
("terrible hands that look peculiar")

10. *Zaraapelta*
("hedgehog shield")

7 BEST PLACES TO FIND A BRAND-NEW DINOSAUR AND GET IT NAMED AFTER YOU

1. Dinosaur National Monument, Utah and Colorado

2. Dinosaur Provincial Park, Canada

3. Liaoning, China

4. Inner Mongolia, China

5. Zhucheng, China

6. Patagonia, Argentina

7. Sahara desert, Africa

9 record breakers

1. Smartest: *Troödon*
2. Fastest: *Ornithomimus* (43 mph)
3. Biggest carnivore: *Spinosaurus* (yes, even bigger than *T. rex*)
4. Biggest: *Amphicoelias fragillimus* (longer than 4 school buses)
5. Biggest egg: *Hypselosaurus*'s (3 times bigger than an ostrich's)
6. Smallest: *Microraptor* (pigeon-size)
7. Most tanklike: *Ankylosaurus*
8. Weirdest: *Deinocheirus mirificus* (look it up!)
9. Longest tooth: *Allosaurus*'s (3.8 inches)

4 WRONGS PUT RIGHT

1. ALL dinos are now thought to have had feathers.
2. Dinosaurs were not as dumb as we once thought.
3. Dinos were not cold-blooded, like most other reptiles are.
4. Dinosaurs were not slow.

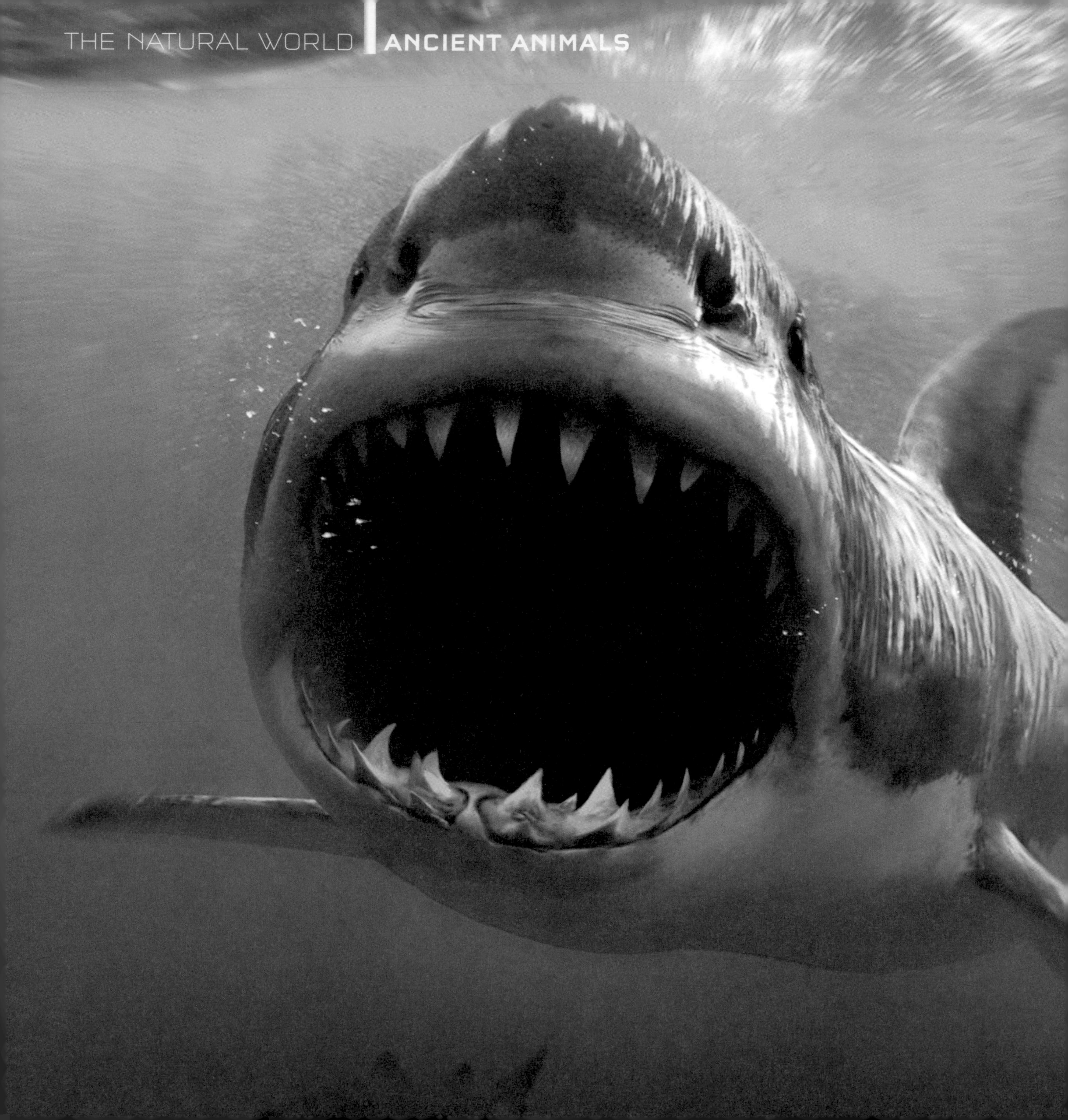

10 ANCIENT ANIMALS

that make polar bears look like Pomeranians

1. Largest insect
Meganeuropsis permiana was a dragonfly with a wingspan of 2.3 feet. It lived among the dinos, 300 million years ago.

2. Largest arthropod
Arthropleura was a prehistoric 8.5-foot-long millipede relative. Just imagine all those wriggly legs!

3. Longest snake
Titanoboa was a 40-foot slitherer, twice as long as snakes today. Luckily, it lived 60 million years ago.

4. Largest land predator
Spinosaurus was a giant meat-eating dino. It was 56 feet long, even bigger than *T. rex.*

5. Largest shark
Megalodon was a 60-foot prehistoric giant with teeth that were 7 inches long.

6. Largest bony fish
Imagine seeing a 55-foot *Leedsichthys problematicus* on the end of your fishing rod!

7. Largest land mammal
Paraceratherium was a gigantic rhino relative that stood 26 feet tall. It weighed more than 5 elephants!

8. Largest flying creature
Quetzalcoatlus had a 40-foot wingspan. This reptile was as big as a small plane!

9. Largest land animal
Amphicoelias fragillimus was a 190-foot sauropod dinosaur. That's longer than 4 school buses.

10. Largest and heaviest animal EVER
The blue whale—not as ancient as the others, but it still lives today!

Woolly mammoth

8 extinct animals that made a BIG impression

1. Woolly mammoth
It was really big.

2. Woolly rhino
It was really big and really hairy.

3. *Smilodon*
This was a colossal saber-toothed tiger.

4. Ground sloth
Sid in the Ice Age films is a ground sloth.

5. Irish elk
It had antlers nearly twice as wide as a moose's.

6. Pterodactyl
This flying reptile could be as big as a small plane.

7. *Meganeura*
This dragonfly was as big as a car tire.

8. *Titanoboa*
This snake was almost as long as a school bus.

7 EXTINCT animals— and it's ALL OUR FAULT

1. Western black rhinoceros
Poached for its horns.

2. Passenger pigeon
Shot and eaten. The last one, named Martha, died at the Cincinnati Zoo in 1914.

3. Carolina parakeet
Last seen in 1910. Its feathers were used on hats.

Mountain gorilla

5

creatures SNATCHED from the JAWS of DEATH

1. The Caspian horse, thought to be extinct since 700 BCE, was discovered alive by the shores of the Caspian Sea in 1965.

2. The Cuban solenodon, a long-nosed rodent, was labeled extinct in 1970—but a specimen was found in 2003!

3. The La Gomera giant lizard re-emerged in 1999 after hundreds of years of supposed extinction.

4. The takahe, a flightless bird lost in the 1800s, reappeared in 1948.

5. The coelacanth, a fish found in 1932, had been thought extinct for 400 million years! That one hid well!

19 AMAZING ANIMALS on the brink of EXTINCTION (SAVE THEM!)

1. Javan rhinoceros
2. Sumatran tiger
3. Erect-crested penguin
4. Atlantic bluefin tuna
5. Mountain gorilla
6. Chinese giant salamander
7. Addax
8. Hawaiian monk seal
9. Bactrian camel
10. Philippine eagle
11. Sawback angel shark
12. Giant panda
13. Radiated tortoise
14. Peacock tarantula
15. Pygmy three-toed sloth
16. Hula painted frog
17. Hainan gibbon
18. California condor
19. Axolotl

4. Dodo
Eaten by animals that people brought to Mauritius.

5. Zanzibar leopard
Deliberately killed because it was thought to be a witch's pet.

6. Great auk
The last known auk in Scotland was executed in 1844 because locals thought that it was a witch—really!

7. Sea mink
Hunted for its fur.

R.I.P

4 bizarro beach finds you'll never believe!

1. In 1992, 28,000 rubber ducks were washed off a ship. People are STILL finding them on beaches!

2. In 2012, an eyeball the size of a softball washed up on a Florida beach. Tests showed that it belonged to a swordfish.

10 disturbing denizens of the briny deep

1. **Darth Vader jellyfish**
   It looks like the helmet!

2. **Ming the clam**
   It was 507 years old when it was found.

3. **Pink see-through fantasia**
   This pretty sea cucumber is pink and transparent.

4. **Tuna**
   It can grow as big as a horse.

5. **Immortal jellyfish**
   It can regenerate itself!

6. **Christmas tree worm**
   It looks just like what it's called.

7. **Anglerfish**
   It can eat animals bigger than itself.

8. **Yeti crab**
   It's really hairy!

9. **Dragonfish**
   It has teeth on its tongue!

10. **Herring**
    Herring talk to one another by passing gas!

3. In 1990, 60,000 Nike sneakers washed off a container ship into the sea. Scientists have been tracking them ever since, to learn more about ocean currents.

4. In 2008, a ghoulish monster landed on a New York beach. It turned out to be a bloated, partially decomposed raccoon.

6 true blue whale tales

1. Its blowhole is big enough for a baby to crawl through.

2. It could blow up 1,250 balloons with a single breath.

3. It's the loudest animal in the sea.

4. The largest land animal, the African elephant, could fit on its tongue.

5. Its heart is the size of a small car.

6. You and 100 of your friends could fit into its mouth.

deadly sea creatures swimming in the same

1. Fire coral
2. Tiger shark
3. Stonefish
4. Saltwater crocodile
5. Box jellyfish
6. Needlefish
7. Puffer fish
8. Geographic cone snail
9. Shorttail stingray
10. Great white shark
11. Nudibranch
12. Crown-of-thorns starfish
13. Portuguese man-of-war
14. Sea lion
15. Sea snake
16. Lionfish
17. Pfeffer's flamboyant cuttlefish
18. Striped pyjama squid
19. Orca
20. Leopard seal

17 things to kiss good-bye when the rainforest disappears

1. Chocolate
2. Chewing gum
3. Bananas
4. Brazil nuts
5. Vanilla
6. Coffee
7. Avocados
8. Cinnamon
9. Mahogany
10. Rubber
11. Many medicines
12. Many perfumes
13. Mangoes
14. Coca-Cola
15. Bamboo
16. Passion fruit
17. Limes

7 rainforest survival tips—they just might save your life!

1. **If you're lost,** follow a river.
2. **Shake your boots out** every day to get rid of deadly critters.
3. **Rub mud on your skin** to keep mosquitoes away.
4. **Don't eat any unknown plants.** If in doubt, fry some ants.
5. **Don't drink river water.** Catch drops from leaves.
6. **Keep your matches dry.**
7. **Avoid large wild animals!**

7 hot, wet stats about the Amazon Rainforest

1. At 2.6 million square miles, **the Amazon Rainforest is the biggest rainforest in the world by far.**
2. It produces 20 percent **of the world's oxygen.**
3. It is thought to have 390 billion **individual trees.**
4. **The Amazon River discharges up to 55 million gallons** of water into the ocean **EVERY SECOND.**

 7 NO-WAY, YES-WAY RAINFOREST CREATURES

1. **Queen Alexandra's birdwing butterfly** is as big as this open book!
2. **The flying fox** is the biggest bat in the world, with a wingspan of almost 5 feet.
3. **The Darwin's bark spider** spins the biggest web in the world—as long as 2 buses.
4. **The okapi** looks like it's half giraffe, half zebra.
5. **The hummingbird** is the fastest flapper. It flaps 80 times a second.
6. **The glass frog** has see-through skin!
7. **The Amazon River dolphin** is pink!

5 rainforest plants that will make you say *YOWZA!*

1. The *Victoria amazonica* water lily's leaves are strong enough to carry a child on the water!

2. The bullhorn acacia tree employs ants to protect it from being eaten—genius!

3. Corpse flowers smell like stinky fish and sweaty socks. Yuck!

4. The pitcher plant looks like a bucket. When small animals fall in, the plant eats them.

5. Strangler figs squeeze trees to death. That's crazy!

5. A quarter of all our medicines come from rainforest plants.

6. About 15 percent of all bird species live in the Amazon.

7. Over 90 percent of all species in the Amazon are insects.

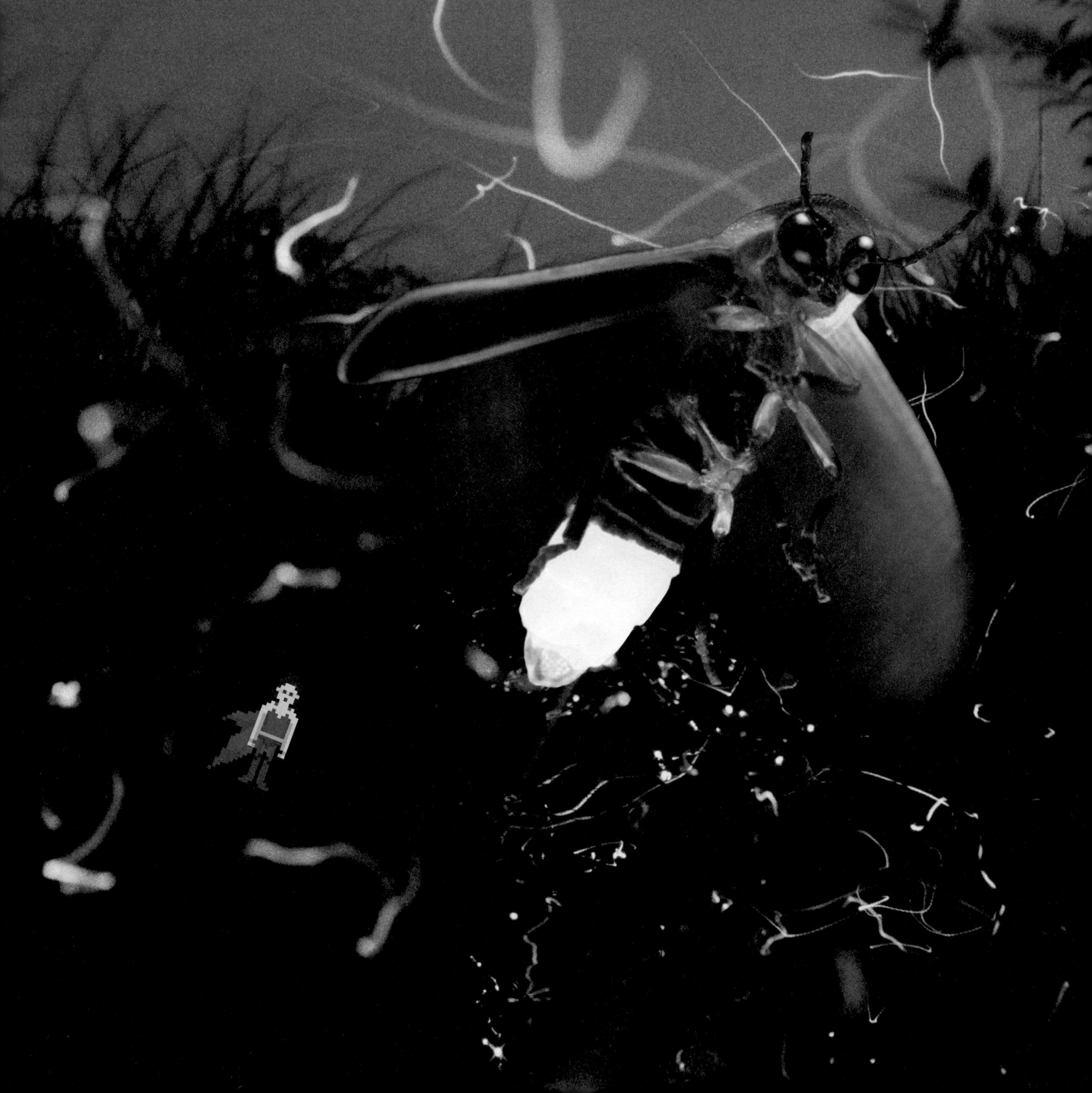

11 superbugs that show that superheroes aren't the only ones with superpowers . . .

1. High jumper
A flea can jump over 200 times its own height.

2. Water walker
Water striders can walk on water. Yes, without sinking.

3. Built-in GPS
Bees have exceptional navigational skills and can always find their way home.

4. Body bulb
A firefly shines light out of its bottom—now that would be fun!

5. Power net
Believe it or not, a spider's silk is one of the strongest materials on the planet.

6. Iron shell
An ironclad beetle has one of the strongest shells in the insect world. You'd have to use a drill to pierce it.

7. Regenerating body
An earthworm can grow back lost parts of its body.

8. Shapeshifter
A caterpillar turns itself into a butterfly. It's like magic!

9. Repellent
Stinkbugs can release smelly liquid to repulse their enemies.

10. Wall walker
Flies can walk across ceilings, and they can move quicker than you can blink. Those are real superpowers.

11. Superstrength
A rhinoceros beetle can lift 850 times its weight. That's like you lifting 9 male elephants.

Anyone need a lift?

9 plants that can really injure you

1. The daffodil, surprisingly, is remarkably poisonous.

2. The giant hogweed will burn your skin. Its sap can cause blindness—though pigs are immune!

3. The angel's trumpet messes with your brain, making you hallucinate, and can kill you.

4. The gympie gympie tree can cause unbearable pain with just a single touch.

5. The tree nettle once killed a man who had simply walked into it!

6. Skunk cabbage will burn your mouth and throat with its foul smell.

7. Apple seeds contain tiny amounts of cyanide . . . but nowhere near enough to kill you!

8. Oleander flowers are so poisonous that the smoke from burning them can kill you.

9. Snakeroot is toxic. If cows eat it, their milk can poison you.

4 BODY PARTS ON CREEPY PLANTS

1. Eyeballs
To watch you . . .

2. Lips
To kiss you . . .

3. Bleeding tooth
To bite you . . .

4. Devil's fingers
To tickle you . . .

6 totally TOP tree facts

1. The dynamite tree explodes with a bang, firing its seeds up to 300 feet away.

2. Bristlecone pines are the world's oldest living things: They can be 5,000 years old!

3. A coast redwood in California named Hyperion is the world's tallest living thing. It is almost 380 feet tall—taller than the Statue of Liberty!

4. 2 trees can provide enough oxygen per year for a family of 4.

5. The manchineel is the most dangerous tree. Its sap can blister your skin. Even standing beneath it in the rain can cause burns!

6. Willows talk to one another! If attacked by a caterpillar, a willow produces a smell that sends a warning to other willows.

What VOLCANIC

Think of a volcano, and you think of fire, destruction, and red-hot lava shooting into the sky. But not all eruptions are like that—are YOU?

1. What color apple would you be?

A	B	C	D
Green, like a Granny Smith.	Yellow, like a Golden Delicious.	Red, like a Red Delicious.	Black, like the one in "Snow White."

2. It's snowing! What do you do?

A	B	C	D
Snuggle up inside with a cup of hot cocoa and a good book.	Go sledding!	Text all your friends to complain about the weather.	Build an igloo, then kick it over.

3. If you were an amusement park ride, what would you be?

ERUPTION are you?

4. It's an emergency! How do you react?

A You push others out of the way, yelling, "Coming through! I got this!"

B You want to help, but you end up wringing your hands and crying.

C You call 911, then kneel by the victim's side and murmur comforting words.

D You pass out.

5. Which Greek god or goddess are you most like?

A Aphrodite, goddess of love.

B Hephaestus, god of fire and iron.

C Apollo, god of light.

D Artemis, goddess of the hunt.

6. In the distance, you hear a loud noise—maybe an explosion! What do you do?

A Rush toward the sound to find out what it is. You have to know!

B Rush toward the sound—what if someone needs help?

C Rush away from the sound—what if something bad is happening?

D Rush away from the sound—what if it's headed toward you?

7. What's your favorite drink?

A A hot drink.

B Soda.

C Ice-cold water.

D A fancy juice.

Got anger issues? Or do you burn slowly? Turn to page 139 to add up your score and find out what volcano you're like!

9 things you can see from space that AREN'T the Great Wall of China

1. Dust storms
2. Wildfires
3. The Great Barrier Reef
4. Volcanic eruptions
5. Air pollution in China

6. The Himalaya mountains
7. Areas of deforestation

8. Blooms of phytoplankton (minuscule ocean plants that live in huge masses)
9. Cities at night, thanks to street and building lights

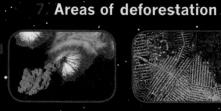

< 10 > earth-shattering discoveries made by Google Earth

1. **A rainforest** on Mount Mabu in Mozambique

2. **Pyramids** in Egypt

3. **A Roman villa** in Italy that is over 2,000 years old

4. **Caves** in an area known as the Cradle of Humankind, in South Africa

5. **The Kamil crater** in Egypt, which was made by a meteorite

6. **An 85-foot structure** used to catch fish in Wales 1,000 years ago

7. **Thousands of tombs** in Saudi Arabia, thought to be 9,000 years old

8. **A pygmy sea horse** off the coast of Australia

9. **A heart-shaped island** in the Adriatic Sea

10. **A hill formation** in Sudan in the shape of luscious lips

6 easy-peasy ways YOU CAN SAVE THE EARTH

1. Recycling 1 can of soda saves enough energy to run a TV for 3 hours.

2. Turning the tap off when you brush your teeth can save 5 gallons of water a day.

3. Telling your parents to pay bills online will save mountains of paper.

4. Riding your bike instead of driving reduces the amount of gas pollution in the air.

5. Avoiding using plastic cutlery prevents the creation of more trash.

6. Refilling a water bottle instead of buying a new one also saves the planet from extra trash.

8 jaw-droppers about our astonishing planet

1. About 9,000 earthquakes occur on Earth each day.

2. Earth's core is as hot as the Sun.

3. Earth is not perfectly round—it's slightly squashed.

4. Earth is about 4.54 billion years old.

5. Lightning strikes Earth 8.6 million times every day.

6. 500 active volcanoes exist on Earth right now.

7. The wind blows 27.7 million tons of dust from the Sahara desert to the Amazon Rainforest annually.

8. The farthest-away photo of Earth ever taken was by *Voyager 1*, from 3.7 billion miles away.

12 it's-raining-*again?* cities

(with average number of storm days per year)

1. **Lakeland, FL** (100)
2. **Fort Myers, FL** (92)
3. **Orlando, FL** (87)
4. **Tampa, FL** (86)
5. **Tallahassee, FL** (83)
6. **Mobile, AL** (79)
7. **Apalachicola, FL** (78)

3 staggering, stay-inside moments in weather history

1. In 2011, after major flooding, people in Ipswich, Australia, were surprised to see sharks swimming up their roads!

2. In 2010, giant hailstones 8 inches in diameter fell in South Dakota.

3. Between 1942 and 2010, Roy C. Sullivan of Virginia was hit by lightning 7 times. And he survived each time!

10 KILLER weather catastroph

that make you realiz how dangerous weat can be

8. Daytona Beach, FL (78)
9. Lake Charles, LA (77)
10. New Orleans, LA (72)
11. Clayton, NM (69)
12. Houston, TX (65)

COLDEST/HOTTEST

1. Vostok Station,
Antarctica
(–129°F on
July 21, 1983)

2. Verkhoyansk,
Russia
(–90°F on
February 7, 1892)

3. North Ice Station,
Greenland
(–87°F on
January 9, 1954)

4. Snag, Canada
(–81°F on
February 3, 1947)

1. Death Valley, CA
(134°F on
July 10, 1913)

2. Kebili, Tunisia
(131°F on
July 7, 1931)

3. Sulaibiya, Kuwait
(128°F on
July 30, 1912)

4. Regina, Canada
(113°F on
July 5, 1937)

1. A flood in China in 1931
killed 1–4 million people.
2. A cyclone in Bangladesh
in 1970 killed 500,000 people.
3. A heat wave in Europe
in 2003 killed 70,000 people.
4. A storm in Venezuela in 1999
killed 15,000 people.
5. A blizzard in Iran in 1972
killed 4,000 people.
6. A hailstorm in Greece
in 1856 killed 4,000 people.
7. A flash flood in Pennsylvania
in 1889 killed 2,209 people.
8. A tornado in Bangladesh
in 1989 killed 1,300 people.
9. A wildfire in Wisconsin in 1871
killed 1,200–2,500 people.
10. A hailstorm in India in 1888
killed 246 people.

1. Ball lightning
Luminous balls, several feet wide, that can explode during storms.

5

stunning weather wonders . . . you won't believe your eyes!

2. Kelvin-Helmholtz clouds
Clouds that look like breaking waves across the sky.

3. Green flash
A green flash seen for a split second above the Sun when it sets.

4. Fire rainbow
A rainbow made visible when the Sun shines across the sky through ice crystals.

5. Snow roller
Huge snowballs blown across the ground by the wind—how cool is that?

2

3

4

5

10 of the freakiest things that have fallen

1. In 1894, a hailstorm in Mississippi surprised locals by dropping a gopher tortoise from the sky!

2. In 2010, hundreds of small white fish called spangled perch dropped out of the sky in Australia.

3. In 2005, people in Serbia hopped around to avoid the shower of thousands of frogs that fell on them.

4. In 1969, golf balls fell from the sky in Florida. They had probably been picked up in a tornado.

5. In 2011, soccer players in the UK were pelted by earthworms.

from the sky

6. In 2001, bright red "blood rain" fell in India for 2 months. Experts think it was colored by algae.

7. In 2012, California experienced piping hot rain!

8. In 2011, the UK enjoyed a fruity windfall when more than 100 apples fell from the sky.

9. In 2013, thousands of spiders fell out of the sky in Argentina—creepy!

10. In 2007, stinky orange, yellow, and green snow fell in Russia. No one knows why. Yuck!

Science &

tech

Awesome!

8 big-bigger-biggest space numbers

1. We are 92,900,000 **miles** from the Sun.

2. The average distance between stars is more than 4 light-years.

3. Right now, on Earth, we are moving 150 miles per second!

4. 1 million Earths could fit inside our Sun.

5. A star in our galaxy is 800 times wider than the Sun.

6. There are about 200 billion stars in the Milky Way.

10 reasons why space discoveries equal immortality!

1. Asteroid 697 Galilea is named after Galileo Galilei (1564–1642).
2. The Hubble Space Telescope is named after Edwin Hubble (1899–1953).
3. Halley's Comet is named after Edmond Halley (1656–1742).
4. The Herschel Space Observatory is named after William Herschel (1738–1822)
5. Leavitt, a crater on the Moon, is named after Henrietta Leavitt (1868–1921).
6. Asteroid 1772 Gagarin is named after Yuri Gagarin, first human in space.
7. Asteroid 6469 Armstrong is named after Neil Armstrong, first human on the Moon
8. The mountains on Titan (Saturn's largest moon) are named after mountains in boo by author J. R. R. Tolkien, including the Misty Mountains, Erebor, and Mount Doom.
9. Asteroid 9007 James Bond is named after the fictional action hero.
10. Galaxy 9Spitch is named after the amateur astronomer, Zbigniew "Zbish" Chetnik, who spotted it in 2014. It was named Spitch after his nickname was misheard by a TV producer!

11 places to see the stars . . . for real (not your backyard)

1. Mauna Kea Observatory, Hawaii
2. Very Large Telescope, Chile
3. South Pole Telescope, Antarctica
4. Yerkes Observatory, Wisconsin
5. Roque de los Muchachos Observatory, Spain
6. Arecibo Observatory, Puerto Rico
7. Australian Astronomical Observatory, Australia
8. South African Large Telescope, South Africa

7. It takes our solar system about 200 million years to complete 1 orbit around our galaxy.

8. Astronomers estimate that there are 1 septillion stars. That's 1,000,000,000,000,000,000,000,000. (But no one knows for sure.)

It's out of this world!

8 ARTS-AND-CRAFTS PROJECTS MADE FROM METEORITES

1. A ring with 9 gems set in meteorite rock
2. A knife
3. A gentleman's watch
4. A bracelet made of meteorite beads
5. A meteorite roller ball pen
6. A lizard sculpture
7. A guitar pick
8. An ancient Buddhist statue

9. Atacama Large Millimeter Array, Chile
10. Indian Astronomical Observatory, India
11. University of Tokyo Atacama Observatory, Chile

10 things on the Moon that you wouldn't expect to find there

1. Bags of pee (from Moon missions)
2. Nail clippers
3. Wet wipes
4. A towel
5. 32-inch tongs
6. A hammer
7. A rake
8. A pair of lunar boots
9. Soap
10. Golf balls (hit by astronaut Alan Shepard with a golf club that he smuggled into space)

8 planets an

1. Mercury: 0
2. Venus: 0
3. Earth: 1
4. Mars: 2
5. Jupiter: 67
6. Saturn: 62
7. Uranus: 27
8. Neptune: 14

12 members of the coole club in history: the only people who have stepped on the Moon

1. Neil Armstrong (1969)
2. Buzz Aldrin (1969)
3. Pete Conrad (1969)
4. Alan Bean (1969)
5. Alan Shepard (1971)
6. Edgar Mitchell (1971)
7. David Scott (1971)
8. James Irwin (1971)
9. John Young (1972)
10. Charles Duke (1972)
11. Eugene Cernan (1972)
12. Harrison Schmitt (1972)

6 Moon secrets

1. Geologist Eugene Shoemaker's ashes were sent to the Moon when he died.

2. The Moon smells like gunpowder.

3. The Moon is moving about 1.5 inches away from Earth every year.

4. An astronaut's footprint could stay on the Moon's surface for millions of years!

5. It would take 133 days to drive to the Moon.

6. You could jump 165 feet high on the Moon.

What ELEMENT of

The periodic table describes the properties of different elements. Can it also tell you something about yourself?

1. How often do you get angry?

A	B	C	D
About once a month.	About once a week.	About once a day.	About once every 15 minutes.

2. "This little light of mine, I'm gonna let it shine!" How brightly does your light shine?

A Like a night-light, which lets you find your way to the bathroom but not very much else.

B Like a well-lit room.

C Like a little star—twinkle, twinkle.

D Like fireworks!

3. Are you strong?

A Yes! I lift weights!

B Yes! I run every day!

C Not really. I can barely lift my own backpack.

D No. I am a weakling.

the PERIODIC TABLE are you?

4. How do you feel about water?

A — I love it! I'm on the swim team, and I go to the beach every chance I get.

B — I hate it! Ugh. Cold, wet, disgusting.

C — I drink it when there's nothing else around.

D — I take showers, sometimes.

5. The zombies are coming! What do you bring to the battle?

A I'm agile, great at quick escapes.

B I fight back, and I fight back hard.

C I'm tricky. I always have a plan.

D I'm a great leader. Follow me!

6. What is one thing that you think you don't have?

A Brains.

B Heart.

C Courage.

D What are you talking about? I'm perfect!

7. What creature do you feel most drawn to?

A A wolf.

B A dragon.

C A whale.

D A horse.

Carbon? Gold? Or something else? Turn to page 139 to add up your score and find out what element you are!

13 supercool space inventions that make life on Earth a lot better

1. Artificial limbs
2. Freeze-dried food
3. Aircraft anti-icing systems
4. Water purification systems
5. Scratch-resistant sunglasses
6. Shoe insoles
7. Remote-controlled ovens
8. Firefighting equipment
9. Enriched baby food
10. Mattress foam
11. Ear thermometers
12. Invisible braces for your teeth
13. Cordless vacuums

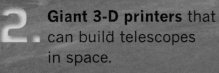

9 out-of-this-world space projects

1. **A giant net** to catch all the garbage that is floating in space.

2. **Giant 3-D printers** that can build telescopes in space.

3. **Humans on Mars** (though they may not come back to Earth).

4. **A Moon base** for astronauts so that they can study space from space.

5. **Capturing an asteroid** and bringing it closer to Earth to study it.

6. **Vacations in space!** (Someone would need to build hotels first.)

7. **A space elevator** to take people to space without rockets.

8. **Space farms** to feed astronauts living in space.

9. **Teeny-weeny satellites** so that there will be less junk in space.

7 THINGS FOUND IN OUTER SPACE

1. Another solar system, with 7 planets
2. A planet made of diamonds
3. A planet of burning ice
4. A massive planet with 100 trillion times more water than Earth
5. Stars traveling through space at trillions of miles per hour
6. The shape of Mickey Mouse's head on Mercury's surface
7. A star 1,500 times bigger than our Sun

happening RIGHT NOW!

4 who-thought-of-that? ways to travel in space

1. Time-traveling wormholes
2. Solar sails (yes, spacecraft with sails)
3. Interstellar ramjets (high-speed nuclear fusion craft)
4. Humans in deep sleep on starships

5 SPACE MISSIONS ON WHICH NO HUMANS WERE HARMED (because there were no humans on board)

1. The *Voyager 1* space probe set off in 1977 and has just now reached the edge of the solar system.

2. *Rosetta* landed on a comet in 2014, after a 10-year journey of 3.7 billion miles.

3. The Mars rover Opportunity has driven 25 miles in 10 years—that's a record for planet travel!

4. *NEAR Shoemaker* was the first probe to land on an asteroid, Eros. It took 160,000 photos on Eros.

5. The *Galileo* space probe left Earth for Jupiter in 1989. It sent back vital information until it self-destructed in Jupiter's atmosphere.

RELOCATING?
WHICH OF THESE 7 EXOPLANETS WOULD YOU CHOOSE TO LIVE ON?

1. Kepler-10c
It's 23 times bigger than Earth—easy to get lost on.

2. GJ1214b
As far as we can tell, this planet is very hot and wet. Bad for your hair.

3. CoRoT-7b
This scorching planet whizzes around its sun in 20 hours. Too speedy!

4. OGLE-2005-BLG-390Lb
This is the coldest planet ever discovered. *Brrrrrr.*

5. Kepler-70b
This scorcher is superclose to its sun, so it's burning hot.

6. TrES-2b
This planet is close to its sun but still really dark. Too scary.

7. Fomalhaut b
This crazy mover zigzags around its sun—very confusing!

7+
inspiring animal astronauts

1. Albert II, rhesus monkey (1949)
2. Patricia and Mike, monkeys (1952)
3. Mildred and Albert, white mice (1952
4. Laika, dog (1957)
5. Belka and Strelka, dogs (1960).
Strelka later had puppies, one of whic
was given to President John F. Kennec
6. Ham, chimpanzee (1961)
7. Félicette, cat (1963)

**Other animals in space have
included rabbits, turtles, ants,
jellyfish, fruit flies, and frogs.**

14 ways that life on the ISS (the International Space Station) is NOT NORMAL

1. No gravity
2. Puffy faces
3. Drinking recycled urine
4. Your food floating away
5. 2 hours of exercise a day
6. Peeing into a suction hose
7. Flaky feet
8. Chicken legs (your legs would get thinner)
9. Sleeping standing up, strapped to a wall
10. Never going out for a breath of fresh air
11. Wearing diapers while on space walks
12. Motion sickness
13. Being woken up by music chosen by crew on Earth
14. Incredible views of Earth

3 what-the-what? COSMIC FACTS TO REMEMBER WHEN YOU ARE IN SPACE

1. There is no sound in space.
2. You can't burp in space.
3. If you fell into a black hole, you would stretch like a rubber band—and then snap!

8 end-of-the-world-as-we-know-it possibilities

1. A black hole eats our galaxy. (One is doing that right now, faster than we thought.)

2. Radiation from a supernova (an exploding star) destroys Earth's atmosphere.

3. A superbig asteroid hits Earth. (NASA says a big one is heading our way in 2032.)

4. The universe is always getting bigger. Too fast, and a sudden rip pulls everything apart.

5. Our galaxy collides with our neighboring galaxy, Andromeda. We lose.

6. A burst of gamma radiation blows apart the planet's atmosphere.

7. Stars get bigger before they die. As the Sun dies, it turns Earth into a fireball.

8. Or the Sun's death destroys Earth's orbit, and Earth plunges into everlasting darkness.

7 most dangerous experiments of all time

3. In the 1660s, Isaac Newton, who discovered gravity, poked his eyeball with a metal spike to see how it affected his vision!

4. In around 1800, Thomas Young attached a metal hook to the back of his eyeball to see how eyes adjust to distances!

5. Daniel Alcides Carrión injected himself with pus to research a serious disease. He died in 1885 before he could figure out how to cure it.

2. Carl Scheele, who discovered oxygen in 1775, liked to sniff and taste his experiments. He died of mercury poisoning.

1. Marie Curie discovered radioactivity, which is used in cancer treatment, in 1898. She died from too much radiation.

5 brain-bustingly bizarre experiments

1. Chicken attraction
Stefano Ghirlanda showed pictures of people to chickens to prove that even chickens prefer attractive faces!

2. That's baaaaa-tty!
An Australian team won a physics prize for testing how sheep might be dragged over different surfaces!

6. Werner Forssmann stuck a tube into his arm and threaded it through his body to his heart in 1929, to prove that doctors could deliver drugs in this way.

7. Humphry Davy inhaled many dangerous gases in his experiments in the 1790s. He discovered laughing gas.

4 brilliant scientists who were ignored, mocked . . . or burned at the stake

1. John Logie Baird was mocked in the early 1900s when he first showed off his invention, the television!

2. Albert Einstein was fired and his books were burned in public during World War II.

3. Giordano Bruno was burned at the stake in 1600 for saying that the Sun is the center of our solar system. He was right.

4. William Harvey was ostracized in the 1600s when he solved the riddle of blood circulation.

3. Catch the vomit!
Stubbins Ffirth swallowed vomit (yuck!) to prove that yellow fever cannot be spread by people.

4. What is belly button lint?
Georg Steinhauser studied 503 pieces of his own belly button lint to find out what it was.

5. Time for a loooong sleep
11 men in Russia were sent to bed for a year to test what it would be like for astronauts to travel through space.

Baaaa!

G-whiz!

7 WAYS TO FEEL THE G-FORCE

1. **Stand still** (1 g)

2. **Ride a roller coaster** (3–4 g)

3. **Drive a Formula One race car** (5 g)

4. **Re-enter Earth's atmosphere from space** (6 g)

5. **Pilot a fighter jet** (9 g)

6. **Be a car crash tester,** like Rusty Haight (10 g)

7. **Train in a centrifuge machine,** like astronauts do (12.5 g)

5 effects of g-force

1. Dizziness
2. Tunnel vision
3. Full loss of vision
4. Loss of consciousness
5. Death

5 GRAVITY FACTS

THAT WILL KEEP YOUR FEET FIRMLY ON THE GROUND

1. Gravity pulls on you all day long. By evening, you have shrunk by about half an inch.

2. The gravity in a black hole is so strong that not even light can escape.

3. Earth's tides are caused by the Moon's gravitational pull on the oceans.

4. Gravity on the Moon is only one-sixth of Earth's gravity.

5. Adjusting to Earth's gravity after space travel is tricky. Astronauts often drop things, forgetting that they won't float.

3 eureka moments! Far-out ways physical laws were discovered

1. **Gravity**
Isaac Newton is hit on the head by an apple—or so the story goes.

2. **Displacement of water**
Archimedes jumps into a bathtub.

3. **Electricity**
Luigi Galvani makes dead frogs move.

5 breakthroughs from seriously smart physicists

1. The accelerating universe
The universe is expanding.

2. Exoplanets
Scientists have discovered planets outside our own solar system.

3. Topological insulators
These materials behave like insulators (they do not conduct electricity) on their insides but do conduct electricity on their surfaces. They might be used to create superfast computers.

4. Quantum teleportation
This might be a first step toward being able to teleport ourselves!

5. The Higgs boson
This particle, only very recently confirmed to exist, is helping us understand how the universe was formed and how it works.

10 DEEPLY DEADLY ELEMENTS
THAT ARE FOUND NATURALLY ON EARTH.
BEWARE!
THEY COULD SERIOUSLY DAMAGE YOUR HEALTH.

4. MERCURY
President Lincoln took mercury as a medicine. If he hadn't been assassinated, the highly poisonous mercury probably would have killed him.

1. BERYLLIUM
If you inhale even tiny pieces of beryllium, it can kill you. It is used in spacecraft and is also found in emeralds.

2. RUBIDIUM
This element catches fire spontaneously and reacts violently in water. It's sometimes used to make purple fireworks.

3. PLUTONIUM
This is considered to be the biggest, baddest element. About 1 pound can kill 2 million people. It is used in nuclear weapons.

1 H Hydrogen 1.00794		
3 Li Lithium 6.941	4 Be Beryllium 9.012182	
11 Na Sodium 22.98976928	12 Mg Magnesium 24.3050	
19 K Potassium 39.0983	20 Ca Calcium 40.078	21 Sc Scandium 44.955912 · 22 Ti Titanium 47.867 · 23 V Vanadium 50.9415 · 24 Cr Chromium 51.9961 · 25 Mn Manganese 54.938045 · 26 Fe Iron 55.845
37 Rb Rubidium 85.4678	38 Sr Strontium 87.62	39 Y Yttrium 88.90585 · 40 Zr Zirconium 91.224 · 41 Nb Niobium 92.90638 · 42 Mo Molybdenum 95.96 · 43 Tc Technetium 97.9072 · 44 Ru Ruthenium 101.07
55 Cs Caesium 132.9054519	56 Ba Barium 137.327	72 Hf Hafnium 178.49 · 73 Ta Tantalum 180.94788 · 74 W Tungsten 183.84 · 75 Re Rhenium 186.207 · 76 Os Osmium 190.23
87 Fr Francium 223	88 Ra Radium 226	104 Rf Rutherfordium 261 · 105 Db Dubnium 262 · 106 Sg Seaborgium 266 · 107 Bh Bohrium 264 · 108 Hs Hassium 277

| 57 La Lanthanum 138.90547 | 58 Ce Cerium 140.116 | 59 Pr Praseodymium 140.90765 | 60 Nd Neodymium 144.242 | 61 Pm Promethium 145 |
| 89 Ac Actinium 227 | 90 Th Thorium 232.03806 | 91 Pa Protactinium 231.03588 | 92 U Uranium 238.02891 | 93 Np Neptunium 237 |

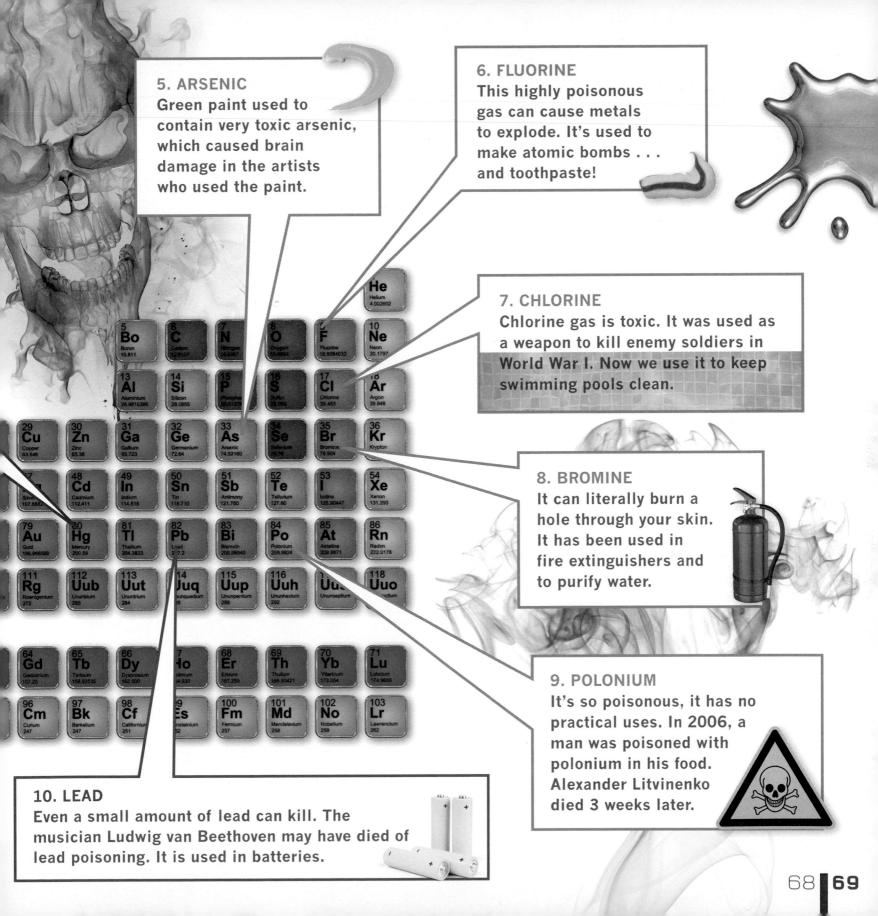

5. ARSENIC
Green paint used to contain very toxic arsenic, which caused brain damage in the artists who used the paint.

6. FLUORINE
This highly poisonous gas can cause metals to explode. It's used to make atomic bombs . . . and toothpaste!

7. CHLORINE
Chlorine gas is toxic. It was used as a weapon to kill enemy soldiers in World War I. Now we use it to keep swimming pools clean.

8. BROMINE
It can literally burn a hole through your skin. It has been used in fire extinguishers and to purify water.

9. POLONIUM
It's so poisonous, it has no practical uses. In 2006, a man was poisoned with polonium in his food. Alexander Litvinenko died 3 weeks later.

10. LEAD
Even a small amount of lead can kill. The musician Ludwig van Beethoven may have died of lead poisoning. It is used in batteries.

11

inventions invented by young (very young!) inventors

1. Braille (Louis Braille, age 15)
2. Popsicles (Frank Epperson, age 11)
3. The trampoline (George Nissan, age 16)
4. Magic Sponge Blocks (Taylor Hernandez, age 10)
5. Wristies, **fuzzy sleeves worn under coats** (KK Gregory, age 10)
6. Magnetic wallpaper (Sarah Buckel, age 14)
7. Earmuffs (Chester Greenwood, age 15)
8. Snowmobiles (Joseph-Armand Bombardier, age 15)
9. Chewing gum (Horatio Adams, age 16)
10. Windsurfing (Peter Chilvers, age 12)
11. Scooters (Walter Lines, age 15)

5

spooky ideas from science fiction, transformed into science fact

1. **An invisibility cloak** can make things seem to disappear—that's spooky!

2. **Time travel** has been accomplished, but only by a few nanoseconds.

3. **Weather control**— scientists can fire laser beams into clouds to make them produce rain or lightning.

4. **Mind control**—a pilot wearing an electronic cap can land a plane using his or her mind.

5. **Tricorders** are handheld scanners that can look for illness in a body.

7

inventio so dum they're brillian

1. Automatic hair cutter

2. Dog scuba-diving apparatus

3. Scream muffler (so you can yell without disturbing your neighbors)

4. Safety coffin, with bell included (so you can't be buried alive)

5. LED flashlight slippers

6. Attachable soda-can handle

7. Extendable arms (for taking selfies)

10

I-want-that!
inventions that sprang from silly mistakes

1. Stainless steel
Harry Brearley was trying to create a gun barrel that wouldn't wear down.

2. Superglue
Harry Coover discovered that a substance he had created stuck to everything just a bit too well!

3. Cornflakes
John Kellogg left some dough out too long but baked it anyway.

4. Microwave ovens
Percy Spencer noticed a chocolate bar had melted in his pocket when he stood next to a machine.

5. Silly Putty
James Wright accidentally poured an acid into an oil— and it bounced!

6. Potato chips
A customer kept sending fried potatoes back to George Crum's kitchen, saying they weren't crunchy enough.

7. Fireworks
A Chinese cook created fireworks 2,000 years ago—probably when they accidentally exploded!

8. Coca-Cola
John Pemberton was trying to invent a headache medicine.

9. Play-Doh
Joseph and Noah McVicker were trying to make a wallpaper cleaner.

10. Matches
John Walker noticed something on the end of a stick. He rubbed it. It caught fire.

tech triumphs of today—that came from Leonardo da Vinci's 500-year-old ideas

1. Crane
2. Alarm clock
3. Gas mask
4. Helicopter
5. Airplane
6. Parachute
7. Glasses
8. Steam engine
9. Telescope

Oh . . . and he painted the *Mona Lisa*, too. What a talented dude!

What WORLD-CHANGING

Inventions have changed the world! From the wheel to the Internet, they have made life more exciting. Which big invention would you be?

1. You're starting a band! What's it called?

The Rowdy Mangoes.	Stinky and the Five Scents.	Txt Mnkys.	Pterodactyls in Love.
A	B	C	D

2. You're going on vacation—what do you want to visit?

A. Old Faithful in Yellowstone National Park.
B. The Eiffel Tower in France.
C. The Taj Mahal in India.
D. Hoover Dam, on the Colorado River.

3. Bake sale! What do you do?

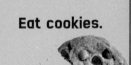

A. Make cookies.
B. Buy cookies.
C. Sell cookies.
D. Eat cookies.

INVENTION are you?

4. A chair just broke. What do you do?

A Sit somewhere else and pretend you didn't notice.

B Prop the chair up on a stack of books.

C Get out the wood glue and some clamps. You can handle this!

D Go to the furniture store and help choose a new chair.

5. Which Harry Potter character do you most identify with?

A Harry. He's the hero!

B Dumbledore. He's the best principal ever!

C Hermione. She's supersmart!

D Hagrid. He's great with animals!

6. If you were a superhero, what would your superpower be?

A Flying through the air.

B Zapping things!

C Turning back time!

D Seeing into people's very souls.

7. Which of these is your favorite?

A A chandelier.

B A flashlight.

C A candle.

D A bonfire.

The telephone? The wheel? Turn to page 140 to add up your score and find out how YOU changed the world!

9 supercool, superfast, HOLD-ON-TO-YOUR-HAT supervehicles

1. **Fastest-moving manned vehicle**
Apollo 10's command module rocketed at 24,791 mph in 1969.

2. **Fastest airplane**
An X-15 fighter plane shot along at 4,520 mph.

3. **Fastest car**
The ThrustSSC whizzes at 763 mph.

4. **Fastest truck**
The Shockwave, a jet-powered truck, zips along at 400 mph.

5. **Fastest boat**
The speedboat *Spirit of Australia* skimmed across water at 318 mph.

6. **Fastest train**
The Shanghai Maglev Train rushes at 303 mph.

7. **Fastest car you can buy**
The Hennessey Venom GT speeds along at 270 mph.

8. **Fastest electric vehicle**
The Ventura Buckeye Bullet 2.5 dashes at 267 mph.

9. **Fastest vehicle on Mars**
The Curiosity rover creeps across Mars at 0.022369 mph. It's pretty slow—but very cool!

10

9

8

7

6

10, 9, 8 . . . COUNTDOWN TO THE FASTEST WAY TO GET TO THE MOON

10. Giant tortoise (136 years)

9. Foot (9 years)

8. Canoe (2 years—if you are an Olympic paddler)

7. Bicycle (120 days—if you are the fastest cyclist on Earth)

6. MV Agusta F4 R 312 motorcycle (52 days)

5. Bugatti Veyron 16.4 Super Sport car (37 days)

4. Eurocopter X3 helicopter (34 days)

3. TGV high-speed train (28 days)

2. Lockheed SR-71 Blackbird aircraft (4.5 days)

1. *Apollo 11* spaceship (4 days, 6 hours, 46 minutes—the quickest-ever journey to the Moon)

BLASTOFF!

10 fuels you really can run a vehicle on (instead of gas)

1. Coffee grounds
2. Cow dung
3. Cooking grease
4. Algae
5. Straw
6. Sugarcane
7. Hydrogen
8. Chocolate
9. Bacon fat
10. Grass

8 brilliant improvements our cars may have in the future

1. **Vehicle-to-vehicle communication**
   Cars will avoid crashes automatically.

2. **Self-driving ability**

3. **Augmented reality windshields**
   Computer images on windshields will give information about surroundings.

4. **Ability to learn**
   Cars will know all about your hobbies and tastes—useful!

5. **Exterior air bags**

6. **Laser headlights**

7. **Self-parking ability**

8. **Solar power**

6 robots that may take over the world but are actually kind of fun

2. **ASIMO**
ASIMO is 4 feet tall and can run at 3.7 mph. It can follow you with its eyes. It's the ultimate assistant!

3. **BigDog**
It is 3 feet long and can run at 4 mph. It's built to travel with soldiers over rough terrain.

1. **Atlas**
This robot is 6 feet tall and has a laser range finder. Developed for the US military, it can withstand missiles.

4. **Bina48**
This humanoid robot has a face that moves, eyes that see, ears that hear, and a mind that can think.

5. **PETMAN**
It's the first robot to walk like a person. It is designed to test chemical protection suits.

6. Valkyrie
This robot is 6 foot 2 and is designed to work alongside astronauts. It stands like a person.

13 SCREEN ROBOTS

1. **WALL-E**
WALL-E

2. **Optimus Prime**
Transformers

3. **Data**
Star Trek

4. **R2-D2**
Star Wars

5. **C-3PO**
Star Wars

6. **The Terminator**
Terminator

7. **The Iron Giant**
The Iron Giant

8. **Daleks**
Doctor Who

9. **Astro Boy**
Astro Boy

10. **Metal Sonic**
Sonic the Hedgehog

11. **Sheriff Not-a-Robot**
The LEGO Movie

12. **Johnny Five**
Short Circuit

13. **Robby the Robot**
Forbidden Planet

6 BRILLIANTLY BRAINY FLYING DRONES

Flying drone

1. **RoboBee**
This tiny robot bee can replace real bees in pollinating crops.
2. **Parcelcopter**
This drone can deliver mail and even pizza!
3. **Camera drone**
This high flier can film sports matches and movies from the skies.
4. **Medical drone**
"Doctor Drone" can carry medical supplies to dangerous areas.
5. **Space drone**
NASA drones can monitor weather from high up in the atmosphere.
6. **Herding drone**
This organizing robot can herd sheep on hillsides. That is pretty cool!

10 real-life cyborg superheroes
(part human, part computer)

1. Where's a USB drive when you need one?
Jerry Jalava lost a finger in a motorcycle accident and had a USB drive implanted in his new finger!

2. No more lost keys
Amal Graafstra popped computer chips into his thumb and fingers. He can now swipe open his front door with no need for keys.

3. The real Iron Man
The US military is working on an exoskeleton suit, like Iron Man's. The suits will give soldiers superhuman strength and senses.

4. Did you miss that? I'll play it back for you!
Canadian filmmaker Rob Spence replaced his lost eye with a video camera. It is wirelessly attached to his computer.

5. Lost? Not anymore!
Electronic engineer Brian McEvoy put a special compass under his skin. Now he has an internal GPS!

6. Was that an earthquake in Japan . . . or was it Hawaii?
Moon Ribas had a sensor put in her arm. Now she can feel vibrations whenever an earthquake occurs—anywhere in the world. Wow!

7. Get me out of here!
In 2002, Kevin Warwick had electrodes attached to his nerve fibers. He can now operate a wheelchair just by thinking about it.

8. Sounds like a cool color
Artist Neil Harbisson is color-blind, so he developed an "eyeborg" that he wears on his head. It converts colors to sounds. Now he can hear colors. How cool!

9. Hands free, ears free
Rich Lee never leaves home without his headphones—they are implanted in his ears!

10. What do you think?
The US Army is experimenting with "thought helmets." They will be able to pass thoughts from one soldier to another through headphones.

4 KOOKY BUILDINGS

1. A house in South Korea is built to look like a toilet! It is now a toilet museum.

2. New Refuge Gervasutti sticks out of a mountain in the Alps. The only way to get to it is by climbing or helicopter.

3. A house in Huainan, China, is in the shape of a giant grand piano and glass violin!

4. The Korowai people in Papua New Guinea have built awesome tree houses in the rainforest canopy, 144 feet in the air!

5 houses that are built without bricks

1. ICE HOUSE
This chilly crash pad in Sweden has to be rebuilt every year because it melts in the summer!

2. PRINTED HOUSE
Architects in the Netherlands are working on the first house created entirely by a 3-D printer.

3. BOTTLE HOUSE
The Wat Pa Maha Chedi Kaew temple in Thailand is made of 1 million glass beer bottles.

4. LEGO HOUSE
In 2009, a full-size LEGO house was built in the UK. 1,000 people used 3.3 million bricks to build it.

5. CRATE HOUSE
A building in Belgium is made of 14,000 beer crates.

14 BIGGEST, LONGEST, TALLEST RECORD-BREAKING STRUCTURES

1. Largest church
Basilica of Our Lady of Peace of Yamoussoukro, Ivory Coast
2. Tallest mosque
Hassan II Mosque, Morocco
3. Largest synagogue
Temple Emanu-El, NY
4. Biggest Hindu temple
Angkor Wat, Cambodia
5. Tallest chimney
At Ekibastuz GRES-2 power station, Kazakhstan
6. Biggest dome
National Stadium, Singapore
7. Longest tunnel
Delaware Aqueduct, NY
8. Longest suspension bridge
Akashi-Kaikyo Bridge, Japan
9. Largest windows
In the Palace of Industry, France (destroyed in 1897)
10. Biggest palace complex
Forbidden City, China
11. Biggest stadium
Rungrado May Day Stadium, North Korea
12. Biggest hotel
Izmailovo Hotel, Russia
13. Largest playground
In the Mall of Dhahran, Saudi Arabia (it can accommodate 2,500 children)

14. **Tallest building:** Burj Khalifa, Dubai

4 INSANELY BAD BUILDING DESIGNS

1. SIZZLER
The Vdara Hotel in Las Vegas, NV, is made of mirrors, which burned guests who lay by the pool!

2. BUCKING BRONCO
The Tacoma Narrows Bridge in Washington swayed so violently in the wind that it collapsed.

3. LEANER
The Leaning Tower of Pisa has been leaning for more than 800 years—but it still hasn't toppled over!

4. SWAYER
The John Hancock Tower in Boston swayed in the wind, making people feel seasick!

4 disaster-proof homes

1. **A hurricane-proof** dome house in Florida
2. **Earthquake-proof** buildings in China that use sticky rice as mortar
3. **Flood-proof** floating houses in Louisiana
4. **A tsunami-proof house** in Washington (water can flow right through it)

What FAMOUS

Where would we be without the amazing inventions of great scientists? Which famous scientist are you most like?

1. Which language would you like to learn?

A Italian.

B German.

C French.

D The language of science! I love controlling the very elements around us.

2. If you were a piece of playground equipment, which one would you be?

A   **B**   **C**   **D**

3. The toilet just broke. What do you do?

A Run away screaming. Ewww!

B Fix it. Everybody knows how a toilet works!

C Research online, then fix it. *Whoosh!*

D Fix it, then flush. Uh-oh. That didn't work—try again!

SCIENTIST are you?

4. A genie gives you one wish. What do you wish for?

A
Something that will improve life for everyone around the world.

B
Something that will improve our understanding of the world around us.

C
Something that will take us to the stars.

D
Something insanely powerful!

5. People describe you as . . .

A Smart and sassy.

B Determined and dynamic.

C Thoughtful and worldly.

D A party animal!

6. You and your friends are going to the movies. What do you want to see?

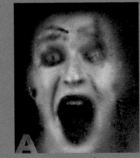
A A horror movie.

B A romance.

C A science fiction film.

D An action movie.

7. Imagine your dream house. What would it look like?

A A prairie dog burrow, cozy but messy.

B A beehive, abuzz with activity.

C A bird's nest, with a bird's-eye view of everything.

D A bear's den, perfect for napping or company.

Einstein? Curie? Turn to page 140 to add up your score and find out what famous scientist you are!

6 COOL (and SERIOUSLY IMPORTANT) NUMBERS

1. Pi

The ratio of the circumference of a circle to its diameter, otherwise known as
3.14159265358979323846264338327950288419716939937510582O9 . . . and so on.
The number is so big that every phone number in the world can be found within it!

7 WHOPPING NUMBERS

1. 1 million = 1,000,000

2. 1 billion = 1,000,000,000

3. 1 trillion = 1,000,000,000,000

4. A googol = 10,000,000,000,000,000,000,00
0,000,000,000,000,000,000,000,000,000,0

5. 1 centillion = 1 followed by 303

6. A googolplex = 1 followed by a googol
you spent your whole life trying!)

7 GET-YOUR-HEAD-AROUND-THESE NUMBERS!

1. **200 million:** the number of insects on Earth for each human being

2. **7 billion:** the number of people on Earth

3. **100 billion:** the number of stars in our galaxy

4. **37.2 trillion:** the number of cells in your body

5. **$60 trillion:** the estimated amount of money in the world

6. **100 trillion dollars (Zimbabwe):** the value of the biggest banknotes ever made

2. The golden ratio
The number 1.6180339887 . . . , which describes perfect proportion in architecture and art.

3. Zero
The number that makes math possible. Yes, really!

4. Absolute zero
The lowest possible temperature. Nothing can be colder than absolute zero.

5. The speed of sound
761 miles per hour
6. The speed of light
186,000 miles per second

7. A zillion = not a real number, but used to describe huge amounts

),000,000,000,000,000,000,000,000,000,000,00
)0,000,000,000,000,000 (1 followed by 100 zeros)

:eros (the biggest number ending in *-illion*)

)f zeros (you couldn't finish writing it even if

7. 352.67 quintillion (352,670,000,000,000,000,000): the number of gallon-size milk containers that would be needed to hold all the water of the world's oceans

3 bet-you-didn't-know computer facts

1. Only 8 percent of the world's currency is actually money that you could put in your piggy bank. The rest exists only on computers.

2. In 1982, the film *Tron* wasn't nominated for a special effects Oscar, because the Academy thought the filmmakers had cheated by using computers!

3. Mary Kenneth Keller was the first woman to earn a PhD in computer science. She had helped develop computer programming. She was a Catholic nun!

12 dates that show that, only 130 years ago, people lived without iPads, laptops, and Google. HOW ON EARTH . . . ?

1. 1888
Charles Babbage's analytical engine is the first computer to calculate complex pi sums. It filled a room!

2. 1936
Alan Turing invents the idea of the modern computer, with a limitless memory.

3. 1951
UNIVAC I and Ferranti Mark 1, as big as desks, are the first computers to go on sale.

4. 1961
The first video game, Spacewar, is invented.

5. 1971
The floppy disk is invented. Now computers can share information.

6. 1976
On April Fools' Day, Apple is launched.

7. 1983
Apple manufactures the first computer with a mouse.

8. 1985
Microsoft launches an operating system called Windows.

9. 1985
The first ".com" URL is registered.

10. 1997
Larry Page and Sergey Brin start Google.

11. 2010
The iPad is launched.

12. The future
We'll control computers with just our thoughts.

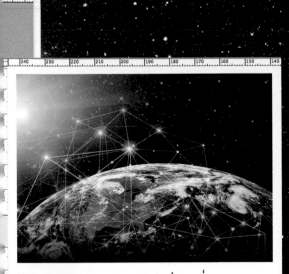

10 countries with the most Internet users

1. China	6. Russia
2. US	7. Germany
3. India	8. Nigeria
4. Japan	9. UK
5. Brazil	10. France

6 sickeningly destructive computer viruses

1. STUXNET
Caused some machines in nuclear plants in Iran to self-destruct.

2. AGENT.BTZ
Attacked government computers at the Pentagon.

3. GAMEOVER ZEUS
Was used to steal passwords, files, and identities.

4. POISONIVY
Allowed the attacker to control the infected computer.

5. MYDOOM
Got into email address books and spread through them.

6. FIZZER
Used email address books to send illegal emails to your friends . . . from you.

Everyday

life

Wow!

10 facts that will give you new respect for your body (and also gross you out)

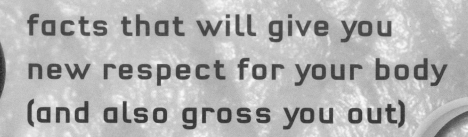

1. If your lungs were spread out flat, they would be the size of a tennis court.

2. Your skin is the biggest and heaviest organ in your body.

3. In your lifetime, you will walk a distance equal to about 4 times around Earth.

4. You will produce enough saliva in your lifetime to fill a swimming pool—yuck!

5. You have between 2 and 4 million sweat glands that produce 2 to 3 pints of sweat daily.

6. You have the same number of hairs that a chimpanzee does!

7. 50 percent of your DNA is the same as a banana's.

8. You will shed 40 pounds of skin in your lifetime, replacing the outer layer every month.

9. In 1 day, your blood travels 12,000 miles, just by going around and around your body.

10. Your nose and ears continue growing throughout your entire life.

7 bodybuilding numbers

1. **206** (number of bones in your body)
2. **Over 600** (number of muscles in your body)
3. **10,000** (number of taste buds on your tongue)
4. **20,000** (number of times you blink each day)
5. **23,000** (number of breaths you take each day)
6. **100,000** (number of times your heart beats each day)
7. **1,000,000,000,000** (number of different scents your nose can smell)

5 unsavory things people have used to make false teeth

1. Elephant tusks
2. Porcelain
3. Wood
4. Hippo teeth (George Washington's dentures were made of hippo teeth)
5. Real teeth stolen from dead bodies on battlefields (yuck!)

1. Urine has been used to make paper.
2. Ancient Romans whitened their teeth with it!
3. It has been used to clean wounds.
4. For many years, it was used to make gunpowder.

6 deeply undignified deaths

1. Greek writer Aeschylus was killed in 455 BCE by a tortoise that an eagle dropped on his head.

2. The ancient Greek Chrysippus died of laughter in 206 BCE after he saw a donkey eating his figs!

3. Chinese poet Li Bai died trying to grasp the Moon's reflection in a river in 762 CE.

4. Béla I, king of Hungary, died in 1063 when his throne collapsed while he was on it!

5. Hans Steininger died when he tripped over his own beard in 1567.

6. Adolf Frederick, king of Sweden, ate himself to death in 1771. He ate lobster, caviar, sauerkraut, and smoked herring with champagne, along with 14 desserts.

R.I.P.

OXYGEN (65%)

HYDROGEN (10%)

CARBON (18%)

28 ELEMENTS YOU NEED TO MAKE A HUMAN—BUT MIX CAREFULLY!

Look out below!

Time to begin my latest tragedy!

8 famously preserved body parts

1. Scientist Isaac Newton's tooth was set in a ring and is now worth thousands of dollars.

2. Russian leader Vladimir Lenin's brain was sliced into 31,000 slivers so that it could be studied.

3. A lock of George Washington's hair is kept in a locket at a Maine museum.

4. Scientist Albert Einstein's eyes were kept by one of his doctors—no one knows why!

5. Composer Frédéric Chopin's heart lies in a crystal jar in Warsaw, Poland.

6. Astronomer Galileo Galilei's middle finger and thumb rest in a museum in Florence, Italy.

7. One of the Buddha's teeth survived the burning of his funeral pyre. It is now in Sri Lanka.

8. Fragments of Abraham Lincoln's skull and the bullet that killed him are in Maryland.

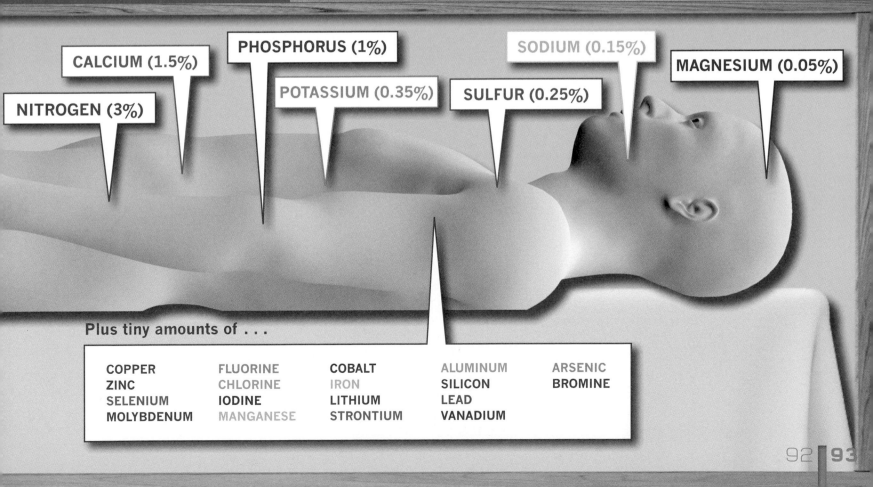

CALCIUM (1.5%)

PHOSPHORUS (1%)

SODIUM (0.15%)

MAGNESIUM (0.05%)

NITROGEN (3%)

POTASSIUM (0.35%)

SULFUR (0.25%)

Plus tiny amounts of . . .

COPPER	FLUORINE	COBALT	ALUMINUM	ARSENIC
ZINC	CHLORINE	IRON	SILICON	BROMINE
SELENIUM	IODINE	LITHIUM	LEAD	
MOLYBDENUM	MANGANESE	STRONTIUM	VANADIUM	

8 EYE-POPPING OPTICAL ILLUSIONS THAT

How many legs do I have?

A VASE OR TWO FACES?

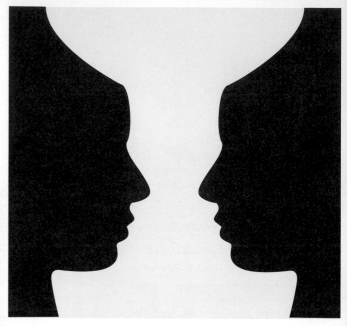

How many triangles are in this picture?

How many people? Do you see the old woman or the young girl?

Moving spirals

WHICH HORIZONTAL LINE IS LONGER?

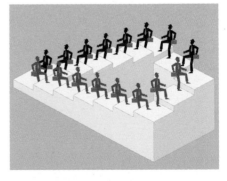

Are the horizontal lines in this diagram straight?

NEVER-ENDING

STAIRCASE

9 helpful ways to say: "That's cool!"

1. Mandarin: *Zhè hěn kù!*
2. French: *C'est super!*
3. Russian: *Eto kruto!*
4. Spanish: *Eso es genial!*
5. Swedish: *Det är coolt!*
6. Finnish: *Että on siistiä!*
7. Indonesian: *Keren!*
8. German: *Das ist cool!*
9. Swahili: *Hiyo ni ya kutisha!*

5 LANGUAGES THAT ARE IN DANGER OF BECOMING EXTINCT (AND WOULD BE FUN TO LEARN)

1. **Magati Ke**
Northern Territory, Australia
3 speakers

10 of the most essential languages to know
(the languages most widely spoken as first or second languages)

1. Mandarin
2. English
3. Spanish
4. Hindi
5. Arabic
6. Bengali
7. Russian
8. Portuguese
9. Japanese
10. German

2. Yuchi
Oklahoma
4 speakers

3. Arem
Vietnam and Laos
40 speakers

4. Omotik
Kenya
Fewer than 50 speakers

5. Wiarumus
Papua New Guinea
160 speakers

5 LUDICROUSLY LONG WORDS

1. Longest word in the English dictionary: pneumonoultramicroscopicsilicovolcanoconiosis. It's a name for a lung disease caused by volcanic ash.

2. Longest place name in the world: Tetaumatawhakatangihangakoauaotamateaurehaeaturipukapihimaungahoronukupokaiwhenuaakitanarahu. It's a hill on New Zealand's South Island.

3. Longest name of a train station: Llanfairpwllgwyngyllgogerychwyrndrobwllllantysyliogogogoch, in Wales.

4. Longest silly word that really is in the English dictionary: supercalifragilisticexpialidocious. This word was invented for the movie *Mary Poppins*. It means "wonderful"!

5. Longest name of a person:
Adolph Blaine Charles David Earl Frederick Gerald Hubert Irvin John Kenneth Lloyd Martin Nero Oliver Paul Quincy Randolph Sherman Thomas Uncas Victor William Xerxes Yancy Zeus Wolfeschlegelsteinhausenbergerdorffvoralternwarengewissenhaftschaferswessenschafewarenwohlgepflegeundsorgfaltigkeitbeschutzenvonangreifendurchihrraubgierigfeindewelychevoralternzwolftausendjahresvorandieerscheinenwanderersteerdemenschderraumschiffgebrauchlichtalsseinursprungvonkraftgestartseinlangefahrthinzwischensternartigraumaufdersuchenachdiesternwelchegehabtbewohnbarplanetenkreisedrehensichundwohinderneurassevonverstandigmenschlichkeitkonntefortplanzenundsicherfreuenanlebenslanglichfreudeundruhemitnichteinfurchtvorangreifenvonandererintelligentgeschopfsvonhinzwischensternartigraum, Senior. He used the name HUBERT BLAINE WOLFESCHLEGELSTEINHAUSENBERGERDORFF, SR., for short!

9 globe-trotting goodies to taste on your travels

1. **Ant larvae** (grubs), found on the roots of agave plants, are eaten in Mexico.

2. **Bird's nest soup,** eaten in China, is made from the nest of the swiftlet. This bird uses its gummy saliva to build its nest!

3. **Surströmming,** fermented herring, is gobbled up in Sweden. It is said to smell more disgusting than any other food.

4. **Mopane worms** are dried out and eaten as a crispy snack in Zimbabwe.

5. **A-ping,** fried tarantula, is eaten and enjoyed like candy in Cambodia.

6. **Kopi luwak** is superexpensive coffee made from beans that have been pooped out by civets, little mammals in Indonesia.

5 things you probably didn't know were in your food

7. *Sannakji* is a Korean dish consisting of pieces of small octopus that are eaten while they are still moving!

8. *Hákarl* is basking shark that is buried and then hung for months, until it has rotted. It is enjoyed in Iceland.

9. **Haggis,** a Scottish specialty, is the heart, liver, and lungs of a sheep, boiled in its stomach.

1. **Arsenic,** a poison, is found in apple juice and brown rice.

2. **Human hair** is used in bread! L-cysteine is a protein found in human hair that makes bread stay fresh.

3. **Beaver urine** is added to vanilla, strawberry, and raspberry ice cream.

4. **Boiled beetle shells** are used to make red food coloring. 70,000 bugs are boiled to produce 1 pound of coloring.

5. **Coal tar** may be used in yellow or orange sodas, chips, or anything cheese flavored.

POP!

7 "biggest-evers"
of foods that you eat every day

1. Hamburger: 2,014 pounds (Minnesota, 2012)
2. Doughnut: 20 feet wide, 3.5 tons (Australia, 2007)
3. Pizza: 50 square feet, 100 pounds (Texas, 2013)
4. Cake: 108 feet high, 30 feet wide (Indonesia, 2008)
5. Strand of pasta: 12,366 feet long (Japan, 2010)
6. Ice-cream cone: 13 feet tall, 1 ton (England, 2012)
7. Bubble-gum bubble: 20 inches wide (Alabama, 2004)

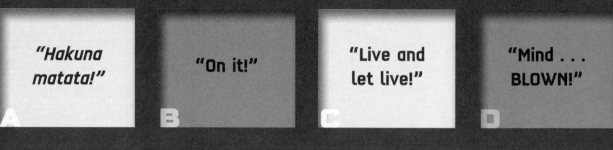

Where should

Big city? Little town? Way out in the country? Are you in the place that's just right for you?

1. What's your personal motto?

A
"Hakuna matata!"

B
"On it!"

C
"Live and let live!"

D
"Mind . . . BLOWN!"

2. It's your birthday! What do you do?

A
Grab a bunch of friends and head to the zoo.

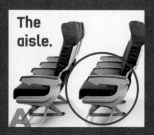

B
Grab a bunch of friends and head to the mall.

C
Grab 2 friends and play video games.

D
Just hang out, watch TV, and have cake with family.

3. Which airplane seat would you pick?

A
The aisle.

B
The window.

C
The center.

D
The pilot's.

4. You've got a time machine! What's your first destination?

A The Stone Age. Things were simpler then.

B Victorian London. Maybe I'll meet Sherlock Holmes! Oh, wait, he wasn't real . . .

C Cape Canaveral in 1969—the year of the first Moon landing!

D The future! It's going to be *amaaaazing*!

5. What is your favorite season of the year?

A Spring. A new beginning!

B Summer. Fun in the sun!

C Fall. Crisp and colorful!

D Winter. Snowballs and skiing!

6. How do you feel about the Empire State Building?

A I wish I could visit!

B I've been there, and the view is incredible!

C Whatever. It's just a big building.

D Eeek, so high up! No way.

7. You're at Mount Rushmore! Who's your favorite?

A George Washington.

B Thomas Jefferson.

C Theodore Roosevelt.

D Abraham Lincoln.

Big city? Way out in the country? Turn to page 140 to add up your score and find out where you should live!

5

of the most expensive foods in the world

1. Alba white truffle
A single specimen of this fungus once sold for $160,000.

2. Almas caviar
2 pounds of sturgeon (fish) eggs can sell for $34,500.

3. Kobe beef
Kobe cows are fed beer and massaged to make their meat tastier—and more expensive!

4. Yubari King melon
In Japan, 2 melons once sold for $23,000.

5. Saffron
60 crocus flowers produce 1 teaspoon of this spice.

6 foods that caused wars

1. Tea
The Boston Tea Party (1773), during which tea was thrown from ships, kick-started the American Revolution.

2. Salt
Venice fought and won a war with other Italian states (1482–1484) for control of salt mines.

3. Cinnamon
The Dutch fought the Portuguese (1602–1663) to access trade routes for importing cinnamon.

4. Corn
Much of the fighting between colonists in North America and Native Americans was over cornfields.

5. Cod
From the 1950s to 1970s, the UK and Iceland were in conflict over fishing areas in the Atlantic Ocean. This was called the Cod War.

6. Sugar
The Spanish-American War (1898) started when the US taxed sugar from Cuba.

5 foods named after people

1. **Peach melba,** for Dame Nellie Melba, an opera singer
2. **Baby Ruth candy bar,** for Ruth Cleveland, the daughter of President Grover Cleveland—not for the famous baseball player Babe Ruth
3. **Margherita pizza,** made in honor of Queen Margherita of Italy (the tomatoes, mozzarella, and basil are the colors of the Italian flag)
4. **Beef Wellington,** for the Duke of Wellington, after he helped win the Battle of Waterloo
5. **Sandwich,** for the Earl of Sandwich, in the UK, after he asked for a meal of meat between slices of bread

7 foods with surprising histories

1. **Lobsters** were once fed to cats and eaten only by the poor.

2. **Chocolate** was drunk by the Aztec people 3,100 years ago.

3. **Peanut butter** also came from the ancient Aztecs.

4. **Ketchup** began as the Chinese *kê-tsiap,* which was a sauce of pickled fish . . . and no tomatoes.

5. **Carrots** were originally purple!

6. **The cotton candy machine** was invented by a dentist!

7. **Ice cream** was invented in China. It was rice and milk packed in snow.

Eat! Eat! Eat!

4 BIG choices to make

1. **There are 7,000** kinds of apple!
2. **An ice cream parlor** in Venezuela serves 860 flavors.
3. **There are around 350** different types of pasta.
4. **There are 7,500** varieties of tomato.

Cucumber, caviar, or cappuccino?

27 CRAZY potato chip flavors

1. Chili pepper and chocolate
2. Seaweed
3. Marmite (yeast extract spread)
4. Blueberry
5. Hot-and-sour fish soup
6. Red caviar (fish eggs)
7. Teriyaki mayonnaise

8. Curry
9. Cajun squirrel
10. Octopus
11. Prawn cocktail
12. Pepsi
13. Cappuccino
14. Avocado salad

15. Salmon sushi
16. Grilled cheese and ketchup
17. Borscht (beet soup)
18. Moose and maple syrup
19. White chocolate and peppermint
20. Chicken and waffles

21. Cucumber

22. Chocolate marshmallow

23. Natural olive oil

24. Wasabi ginger

25. Scallops with garlic butter

26. Cinnamon bun

27. Bacon, eggs, toast, and tomato

7 unusual coins that have stories to tell!

1. Concorde
Each 5-pound coin from the island of Tristan da Cunha has a tiny piece of the Concorde airplane in it.

2. Jonathan the tortoise
The 5-pence coin from the island of Saint Helena shows Jonathan the giant tortoise—the world's oldest living reptile.

3. Pyramid
A triangular-shaped coin was made on the Isle of Man, in the UK, to commemorate Tutankhamen.

4. Mammoth
Every 1,000-franc coin from the Ivory Coast has a tiny piece of mammoth in it.

5. Surfer
The Republic of Palau made a coin with a surfer on it. When you rub it, it smells like the ocean!

6. Star Wars
The Pacific island of Niue made two Star Wars coins: a coin with Princess Leia and Luke Skywalker on it, and another with R2-D2 and C-3PO.

7. Crazy shapes!
Somalia makes coins in interesting shapes—like cars, wild animals, and even electric guitars.

10 OF THE MOST VALUABLE NATURAL MATERIALS ON EARTH

1. Rhodium
2. Platinum
3. Gold
4. Ruthenium
5. Iridium

6. Osmium
7. Palladium
8. Rhenium
9. Silver
10. Indium

5 ordinary things that were used as money (you're a salt millionaire!)

1. STONES
On the Pacific island of Yap, stones were used as money. Some were 12 feet high! Those are hard to slip into your pocket!

2. SALT
The ancient Romans loved salt and were often paid in it. The word *salary* comes from payments made in sa

3. CANDY
In 2008, Argentina ran short of coins. Shops gave out candy rather than their precious few coins!

4

RIDICULOUSLY EXPENSIVE TOYS YOU COULD BUY IF YOU SAVED YOUR ALLOWANCE . . . FOR YOUR ENTIRE LIFE

1. A Hot Wheels car made of diamonds ($140,000)

2. A Barbie doll wearing a real diamond necklace ($302,500)

3. A Monopoly board encrusted with gold and jewels ($2 million)

4. A soccer ball covered in diamonds ($2.95 million)

4. BEAVERS
In colonial times, Native Americans traded valuable beaver skins to Europeans.

5. COWRIE SHELLS
Shells were once used as money all over the world. They are still used on an island off Papua New Guinea.

What JOB is right

You can be anything you want! But what's right for you? Let this quiz help you figure it out!

1. What's the last thing you made?

A A work of art.

B Money.

C A gift for my friend's birthday.

D A weird face in my school picture.

2. True or false: You have lots of friends.

A Somewhat false! I have just a few close friends.

B Somewhat true! I have many friends, but I like being on my own, too.

C True! I'm just not happy unless I'm around other people.

D False! I'm really shy till I get to know someone.

3. When you were younger, what was your favorite book?

A *The Little Engine That Could.*

B *The Story of Babar.*

C *Madeline.*

D *The Lorax.*

4. Do you like to travel?

A Yes! The more exotic, the better!

B Only if I'm going to a familiar place, like my cousins' house.

C No, I really like my own house and my own stuff, thank you very much.

D I like to be in a new place, but the car ride or plane ride to get there is so booooring.

5. Do you keep up with the news?

A Yes, I watch the news every night with my parents.

B I listen to school announcements sometimes. Does that count?

C I look at a news site online once in a while.

D Nope, I know everything I need to know about the world!

6. You won the lottery! What do you do with the money?

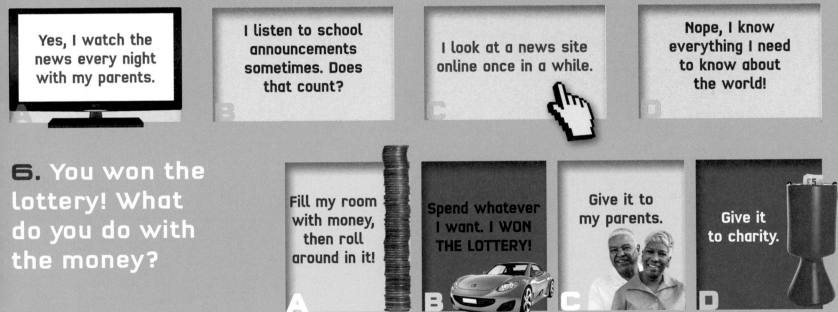

A Fill my room with money, then roll around in it!

B Spend whatever I want. I WON THE LOTTERY!

C Give it to my parents.

D Give it to charity.

7. You are a superhero! What's your ride?

A Batmobile, Catmobile, Ratmobile . . . whatever matches my superhero name.

B An invisible airplane.

C A motorcycle.

D I don't need a ride! I can fly, duh!

Dancer? Dentist? Turn to page 141 to add up your score and find out what job is right for you!

B all-time worst jobs (stay in school, kids!)

1. The groom of the stool wiped the monarch of England's bottom!

2. Leech collectors let leeches (bloodsucking worms once used by doctors) attach to their legs.

3. A punkah wallah was a servant who fanned his boss all day by hand.

4. A tosher scavenged through sewers for treasures.

5. Chimney sweep children were sent all the way up chimneys to clean them.

6. A fuller stomped on sheep fleeces in vats of pee and lime.

7. A food taster had to test a king's food for poison—by eating it.

8. A gong farmer cleaned sewers— that's seriously stinky!

7 dream jobs you'll wish you had

1. Zombie (employed to scare tourists at the London Dungeon)

2. Ice cream taster

3. Video game tester

4. Water slide tester

5. Duvet tester

6. Chocolate taster

7. Great Barrier Reef caretaker

10 of the weirdest jobs you can do today

1. Bicycle fishers
They fish bikes out of canals in Amsterdam, the Netherlands.

2. People pushers
They push people onto crowded trains in Japan.

3. Professional mourners
They weep at funerals!

4. Gum busters
They remove chewing gum from streets.

5. Ear cleaners
Guess what they do.

6. Ostrich babysitters
They keep baby ostriches from pecking one another to death.

7. Dice inspectors
They make sure that there are no cheat dice in casinos.

8. Golf ball divers
They dive for stray balls in golf course waters.

9. Pet food tasters
Yuck!

10. Odor judges
They sniff people's armpits to see if deodorants work!

8 animals that work hard—so we don't have to!

1. **Carrier pigeons** are used to carry messages.

2. **Civets** swallow and then poop out coffee beans, which we grind and drink.

3. **Guide dogs** help people who can't see.

4. **Dolphins** are used in Brazil to lure fish into nets.

5. **Golden eagles** are used in Kazakhstan to hunt and catch animals.

6. **Mine detection dogs** sniff out explosives.

7. **Cormorants** are trained to catch fish in Asia.

8. **Pigs** sniff out truffles—a type of fungus that we eat.

PASSPORT

7

BRAVE FEMALE EXPLORERS

1. Gudrid Thorbjarnardottir was on the first European boat to reach the Americas, in about 1000 CE.

2. Jeanne Baret was the first woman to sail around the world, starting in 1766. She disguised herself as a man.

3. Sacagawea helped explorers Lewis and Clark travel across North America in 1804–1806.

4. Annie Londonderry cycled around the world with only a revolver in 1894–1895.

5. Valentina Tereshkova was the first woman in space, in 1963.

6. Junko Tabei was the first woman to climb Mount Everest, in 1975.

7. Laura Dekker became the youngest person to sail around the world solo, in 2012. She was 16.

PACK YOUR BAGS!

14 WILDLY EXCITING PLACES STILL TO EXPLORE

14. Mars

1. Mariana Trench, Pacific Ocean
2. Gangkhar Puensum mountain, Bhutan
3. Antarctica
4. Cloud forests of Colombia
5. Papua New Guinea
6. Namib Desert, Africa
7. Eastern Kamchatka Peninsula, Siberia
8. Flooded Yucatán cenotes (caves), Mexico
9. Amazon Rainforest, South America
10. Krubera Cave, Georgia
11. Mansarovar Lake, China
12. Congo River basin, Africa
13. Dark side of the Moon

WAY TO M. EVEREST B.C.

Everest records

1. **First known to summit (reach the top)**
Edmund Hillary and Tenzing Norgay in 1953

2. **Highest brawl**
Two Chilean teams raced to summit in 1992. They had a fight at the top!

3. **First disabled person to summit**
Tom Whittaker, with an amputated foot, in 1998

4. **First to descend by snowboard**
Marco Siffredi in 2001

5. **First (and only) blind person to summit**
Erik Weihenmayer in 2001

 6. **First to get married on Everest**
Pem Dorjee and Moni Mulepati in 2005

7. **First to paraglide over the top**
Bear Grylls and Gilo Cardozo in 2007

8. **Youngest to summit**
Jordan Romero, age 13, in 2010

9. **Oldest to summit**
Yuichiro Miura, age 80, in 2013

5 around-the-world speedsters (let's go global!)

1. **First to travel around the world**
Starting in 1519, it took Ferdinand Magellan's crew almost 3 years by ship.

2. **Fastest by foot**
Tom Denniss ran a marathon a day for 622 days, finishing his round-the-world tour in 2013. He went through 17 pairs of shoes!

3. **Fastest by bike**
In 2010, Alan Bate cycled around the world in 126 days.

4. **Fastest by hot-air balloon**
In 2002, Steve Fossett took 13 days and 3 minutes to fly nonstop around the world.

5. **Fastest by plane**
57 hours and 54 minutes is the record for a nonstop plane ride around the world, set in 2010.

10 EXTREME SURVIVORS
who are very, very lucky to still be alive

1. Top trekker
In 2008, Ed Stafford began walking down the Amazon River—and didn't stop for 2 years.

2. Deep caver
Robbie Shone spent 94 hours in a cave over half a mile underground. He took amazing photographs of it.

3. High jumper
In 2014, Alan Eustace jumped out of an airplane that was 25 miles high. He fell at 824 mph.

4. Storm chaser
Sean Casey drives into tornadoes and films them from the inside!

5. Free climbers
In 2015, Tommy Caldwell and Kevin Jorgeson climbed El Capitan, a 3,000-foot-tall rock formation in Yosemite National Park . . . without ropes.

6. Volcano man
G. Brad Lewis has risked frying his camera—and himself—to photograph fiery molten lava exploding from volcanoes.

7. Ultimate explorer
Ranulph Fiennes visited both poles, climbed Mount Everest, and, at age 59, completed 7 marathon runs in 7 days.

8. Bat man
In 2012, Gary Connery jumped out of a helicopter at 2,400 feet—WITHOUT A PARACHUTE. . .

9. Ice swimmer
Lynne Cox swam through Antarctic waters in just a swimsuit for 25 minutes. Most people would have died after 5 minutes.

10. Free diver
Stig Åvall Severinsen is a champion free diver. He can hold his breath for 20 minutes.

14 BIG record setters in the US

1. Biggest museum complex
Smithsonian Institution (Washington,

2. Longest road
Pan-American Highway (it stretches from Alaska to Argentina!)

3. Biggest hot-air balloon festival
Albuquerque International Balloon Fiesta (New Mexico)

4. Largest space observatory
Mauna Kea Observatory (Hawaii)

5. Tallest trees
Redwoods (California)

6. Biggest indoor aquarium
Georgia Aquarium

7. Largest landlocked harbor
San Francisco (California)

5 state claims to fame

1. Alaska has a longer coastline than any other US state. It's longer than all the other state coastlines combined.

2. New Jersey

3. Texas is the home of NASA, the center for space exploration.

4. Maine

5. Virginia is the birthplace of the most US presidents, with 8.

8. **Biggest company**
Walmart (based in Arkansas)

9. **Longest deep canal system**
Saint Lawrence Seaway
(New York)

10. **Biggest library**
Library of Congress
(Washington, D.C.)

11. **Biggest natural bridge**
Rainbow Bridge National
Monument (Utah)

12. **Longest cave system**
Mammoth Cave (Kentucky)

13. **Largest waterfall**
Niagara Falls (New York)

14. **Biggest bakery**
Nabisco bakery (Illinois),
where Oreo cookies are made

STATE SECRETS OF HAWAII

1. **Hawaii is the only state** with a tropical rainforest.

2. **Iolani Palace** is the only royal palace in the US.

3. **Hawaii is the only state** made up entirely of islands.

4. **Hawaii is the only state** that is getting bigger (due to lava from volcanic eruptions).

5. **No building in Hawaii** is allowed to be taller than a palm tree.

6. **The Hawaiian islands** are the tops of mountains in the tallest range on the planet.

7. **From east to west,** Hawaii is the widest state in the US.

21

states with animals on their flags

1. **California**
(bear)

2. **Illinois, 3. Iowa, 4. New York,**
5. North Dakota
(eagle)

6. **Missouri**
(bears and eagle)

7. **Delaware**
(ox)

8. **Idaho**
(elk)

9. **Minnesota, 10. New Jersey,**
11. South Dakota
(horse)

12. **Kansas**
(horses and American bison)

13. **Pennsylvania**
(horses and eagle)

14. **Wyoming**
(eagle and American bison)

15. **Louisiana**
(pelicans)

16. **Maine**
(moose)

17. **Michigan**
(elk, moose, and eagle)

18. **Oregon**
(oxen, eagle, and beaver)

19. **Utah**
(bees and eagle)

20. **Vermont**
(cow and deer)

21. **Wisconsin**
(badger)

13 REASONS TO MOVE THIS YEAR

1. Want to discover a brand-new dinosaur?
Head to Dinosaur Provincial Park, in Alberta, Canada.

2. Love chasing tornadoes?
Move to Tornado Alley, in the US Midwest.

3. Want to sweat?
Dallol, Ethiopia, is the hottest inhabited place.

4. Prefer the cold?
Oymyakon, Russia, is the coldest inhabited place.

5. Need to get away?
Head to the island of Tristan da Cunha, the inhabited place farthest away from any other.

6. Hate the sea?
Move to Xinjiang, China, which contains the spot farthest from any ocean.

7. Love the sea?
Join the Bajau people in the Philippines. They live on floating boats and rarely step on land.

8. Want to sing in the rain?
Head to Mawsynram, India. It gets the most rainfall.

9. Enjoy looking down?
Relish the view from La Rinconada, Peru, the highest city in the world.

10. Love nighttime?
Spend October to February in Longyearbyen, Norway. It's dark for the whole 5 months.

11. Want a lot of neighbors?
Go to Monaco. It has the most people squished into one area.

12. Need more space?
Move to Mongolia, the country with the fewest people per square mile.

13. Want to float?
Train as an astronaut and rocket to the International Space Station.

Home
NEXT EXIT ↗

6 lost cities—that we've found!

1. Cliff Palace, Colorado
This amazing Pueblo city was built into a cliff in the 1200s and rediscovered in 1888.

2. Pavlopetri, Greece
This 5,000-year-old city was found underwater. It is thought to have been destroyed by an earthquake.

3. Tikal, Guatemala
This huge ancient Mayan city was found deep in the rainforest.

4. Machu Picchu, Peru
This 15th-century Incan city was discovered high up in the mountains, completely hidden under plants, in the early 20th century.

5. Angkor, Cambodia
This city of 1,000 temples once stretched over 390 square miles. Laser technology has recently revealed what the whole city would have looked like 900 years ago.

6. Pompeii, Italy
This ancient Roman city was destroyed by a volcano. The ash preserved the city—and its people—in amazing detail.

8 GREAT things about GREAT cities

1. Most skyscrapers
With 302 skyscrapers, Hong Kong has the most. (New York City has 235.)

2. Shortest
In Paris, France, buildings cannot be taller than 6 stories, so that each house gets sunlight.

3. Most bicycles
1 million bicycles ride along 250 miles of bike lanes in Amsterdam, the Netherlands.

9 longest subways for getting
1. Seoul Subway, South Korea: 584 miles
2. Shanghai Metro, China: 290 miles
3. Beijing Subway, China: 283 miles
4. London Underground, UK: 250 miles
5. New York City Subway, New York: 229 miles

4. Wettest
Venice, Italy, is built on 117 small islands, all connected by bridges.

5. Most haunted
Edinburgh, Scotland, is filled with creepy vaults and ghostly ghouls.

6. Most people
There are over 37 million people living in Tokyo, Japan.

7. Windiest
Powerful winds gust between the 2 islands of New Zealand and whistle through its capital, Wellington.

8. Highest
La Paz, Bolivia, stands 11,913 feet above sea level—that's high!

5 top earthy-crunchy cities

1. **Reykjavík, Iceland,** will run completely on natural sources by the year 2050.

2. **Portland, Oregon,** is famous for its green spaces and its food, which is produced mostly locally.

3. **Curitiba, Brazil,** has grass-eating sheep that roam the entire city, keeping it tidy.

4. **Malmö, Sweden,** includes one area that is powered only by sunlight, wind, and water.

5. **Vancouver, Canada,** is the world's biggest user of water-powered electricity—so there is hardly any pollution.

round underground

6. Moscow Metro, Russia: 197 miles

7. Tokyo Metro and Toei Subway, Japan: 193 miles

8. Madrid Metro, Spain: 182 miles

9. Guangzhou Metro, China: 144 miles

6 most godlike Olympians

1. **Michael Phelps, US**
22 medals (swimming)

2. **Larisa Latynina, USSR**
18 medals (gymnastics)

3. **Nikolai Andrianov, USSR**
15 medals (gymnastics)

4. **Edoardo Mangiarotti, Italy**
13 medals (fencing)

5. **Takashi Ono, Japan**
13 medals (gymnastics)

6. **Boris Shakhlin, USSR**
13 medals (gymnastics)

8 extreme sports that will make your mother scream

1. **BASE jumping:** parachuting off high structures or cliffs

2. **Free soloing:** rock climbing with no safety ropes

3. **Wingsuit flying:** skydiving while wearing a crazy suit with wings

4. **Ice climbing:** climbing up glaciers, icy rocks, and frozen waterfalls

5. **Volcano boarding:** yes, surfboarding down the sides of volcanoes

6. **Cave diving:** scuba diving in pitch-black underwater caves

7. **Kite skiing:** skiing while attached to a powerful kite

8. **Creeking:** kayaking down steep, superdangerous rocky rivers

8

sports for animal athletes

1. Horse racing
2. Camel racing
3. Greyhound racing
4. Dogsledding
5. Pigeon racing
6. Polo (on horses)
7. Elephant polo
8. Rodeo (horse riding, bull riding, steer wrestling, calf roping)

5 that-can't-be-healthy sports record holders

1. Dan Magness of the UK kept a soccer ball up for 26 hours, using just his feet, legs, shoulders, and head.

2. Christopher Irmscher of Germany ran the 100-meter hurdles in 14.82 seconds—while wearing flippers.

3. Thaneswar Guragai of Nepal bounced a basketball 444 times in 1 minute.

4. 400 people from 31 countries held hands in a skydive free fall for more than 4 seconds.

5. Katsumi Tamakoshi of Japan completed the fastest 100-meter run ON ALL FOURS in 15.86 seconds.

15 bouncing balls

1. Quidditch quaffle
(12.0 inches)

2. Basketball
(9.4 inches)

3. Soccer ball
(8.7 inches)

4. Tenpin bowling ball
(8.5 inches)

5. Croquet ball
(3.6 inches)

1 record that has never been broken

In 1974, a 64-year-old man named Mike Austin drove a golf ball 515 yards from the tee on a golf course in Las Vegas, NV. No one has ever hit a ball farther.

SMASH THAT BALL!

9 of the fastest balls in sports

1. Golf ball (211 mph)

2. Jai alai ball (188 mph—this is commonly thought to be the most dangerous sports ball in the world)

3. Squash ball (175 mph)

4. Tennis ball (164 mph)

5. Soccer ball (131 mph)

6. Field hockey ball (114 mph)

7. Baseball (108 mph)

8. Cricket ball (100 mph)

9. Ping-Pong ball (70 mph)

WEIRD BUT TRUE
A badminton shuttlecock isn't a ball at all, but it beats all balls with its fastest recorded speed—306 mph!

7. Field hockey ball (2.9 inches)

8. Cricket ball (2.8 inches)

9. Tennis ball (2.6 inches)

10. Jai alai ball (2.1 inches)

11. Billiard ball (2.0 inches)

12. Golf ball (1.7 inches)

13. Ping-Pong ball (1.6 inches)

14. Squash ball (1.6 inches)

15. Quidditch snitch (1.0 inch)

5 Harry Potter LOCATIONS TO VISIT

1. Platform 9 3/4, King's Cross station, London, UK
2. Reptile House, London Zoo, UK
3. Glenfinnan Viaduct, Scotland, UK (the Hogwarts Express runs across this bridge)
4. Alnwick Castle, Northumberland, UK (one of several filming locations for Hogwarts)
5. Warner Bros. Studio Tour, London, UK

5 genius Star Wars sound effects

1. Bicycle chains dropped on concrete: AT-AT walkers

2. The hum of an old TV set and projector: lightsabers

3. Walrus and other animal sounds: Chewbacca

4. The sound of highway traffic through a vacuum cleaner pipe: Luke's landspeeder

5. Tibetan, Mongolian, and Nepali, layered and altered: the Ewok language

Humm
Humm
Humm
Humm
Humm

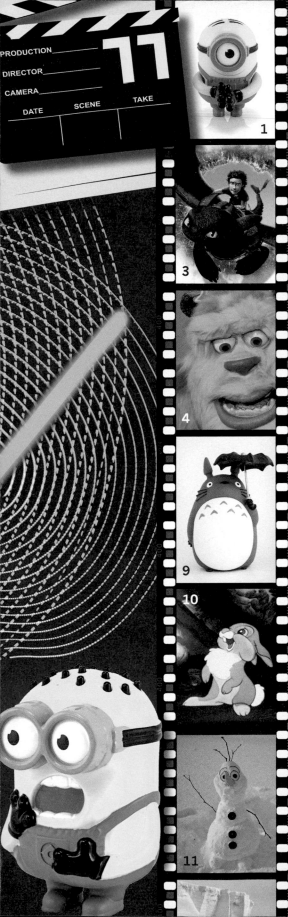

CUTE ANIMATED CHARACTERS YOU WOULD LOVE TO HAVE AS PETS

1. **The Minions,** Despicable Me series

2. **Scott "Squishy" Squibbles,** *Monsters University*

3. **Toothless,** How to Train your Dragon series

4. **Sulley,** *Monsters, Inc.* and *Monsters University*

5. **Scrat,** Ice Age series

6. **Pascal,** *Tangled*

7. **Dug,** *Up*

8. **Po,** Kung Fu Panda series

9. **Totoro,** *My Neighbor Totoro*

10. **Thumper,** *Bambi*

11. **Olaf,** *Frozen*

18 OF THE HIGHEST-GROSSING MOVIES OF ALL TIME

1. *Avatar* (2009)

2. *Titanic* (1997)

3. *Marvel's The Avengers* (2012)

4. *Harry Potter and the Deathly Hallows: Part 2* (2011)

5. *Frozen* (2013)

6. *Iron Man 3* (2013)

7. *Transformers: Dark of the Moon* (2011)

8. *The Lord of the Rings: The Return of the King* (2003)

9. *Skyfall* (2012)

10. *Transformers: Age of Extinction* (2014)

11. *The Dark Knight Rises* (2012)

12. *Pirates of the Caribbean: Dead Man's Chest* (2006)

13. *Toy Story 3* (2010)

14. *Pirates of the Caribbean: On Stranger Tides* (2011)

15. *Jurassic Park* (1993)

16. *Star Wars: Episode I The Phantom Menace* (1999)

17. *Alice in Wonderland* (2010)

18. *The Hobbit: An Unexpected Journey* (2012)

7 epic movie lines to quote

"You underestimate the power of the dark side." —Darth Vader, *Return of the Jedi*

"Sorry! I don't want any adventures, thank you. Not today." —Bilbo Baggins, *The Hobbit*

"To infinity and beyond!" —Buzz Lightyear, Toy Story series

"Hey, pea-brain!" —Ron Weasley, *Harry Potter and the Sorcerer's Stone*

"Hakuna matata." —Timon and Pumbaa, *The Lion King*

"Adventure is out there!" —Ellie, *Up*

"When 900 years old you reach, look as good you will not." —Yoda, *Return of the Jedi*

9 totally deadly superhero weapons

1. Iron Man's armor
Tony Stark's suit has built-in weapons and allows him to fly.

2. Wolverine's claws
There are blades in his knuckles!

3. Thor's hammer
Made from the core of a star, this hammer summons lightning.

4. Green Lantern's power ring
The ring can create any weapon that the wearer imagines.

5. Hawkeye's bow
This bow is multitasking and collapsible.

6. Spider-Man's web-shooters
Devices on his wrists shoot out strong, sticky spiderwebs.

7. Batman's batarangs
He has bat-shaped throwing weapons!

8. Captain America's shield
The indestructible shield protects him and can also be hurled at enemies.

9. Daredevil's billy club
This multipurpose stick can be us as a baton or a grappling hook o can be hurled at enemies.

10 superhero movie series

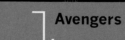

1. Avengers   **2.** Batman   **3.** Spider-Man   **4.** Iron Man

1. "With great power comes great responsibility."
—Spider-Man

2. "I'm here to fight for truth, and justice, and the American way."
—Superman

3. "Oh, no . . . this is Earth, isn't it?"
—Thor

4. "You know, sometimes when you cage the beast, the beast gets angry."
—Wolverine

5. "*Now* you wanna get nuts? Come on! Let's get nuts!"
—Batman

6. "Cats come when they feel like it. Not when they're told."
—Catwoman

6 grrrr-oovy facts you probably didn't know about Wolverine

1. **Wolverine** was almost called "the Badger."

2. **Wolverine's claws** were originally part of his gloves.

3. **He first appeared** in the comic book *The Incredible Hulk*.

4. **Hugh Jackman** has played Wolverine in 7 movies.

5. **Because of his healing abilities,** no one knows Wolverine's age.

6. **Wolverine's bones** are plated in adamantium, an indestructible (fictional) metal.

5. X-Men   6. Superman   7. Thor   8. Fantastic Four   9. Hulk   10. Teenage Mutant Ninja Turtles

How long would

Hurricanes! Crash landings! Snowstorms! How long would you survive if a disaster happened?

1. True or false: You judge people by the shoes they are wearing.

A False! Never!

B False! Well, hardly ever.

C True! All the time!

D True! But I'm embarrassed to admit it. Does that count for anything?

2. How many zombies could you fight off?

A Maybe 1, if it was small and weak.

B At least 3. I've totally got this.

C The fast kind or the slow kind?

D That depends on the weapons at my disposal.

3. Your house is on fire! What do you take?

A My dog.

B The clothes on my back.

C My cell phone.

D Tomorrow's homework.

you SURVIVE?

4. Could you build a fire?

A Yes, in the fireplace, with a dry-as-toast log and a full box of matches.

B Yes, I've done it on camping trips.

C Yes, I think I could.

D No way. I can barely turn on the stove.

5. What do you do when you're packing for a vacation?

A I overpack. I need a burro to carry all my stuff!

B I underpack. I never seem to have enough underwear . . .

C I research the place I'm going, then pack exactly what I'll need.

D I research the place I'm going, then pack what I'll need, then get a burro to carry it all.

6. If you were a mythological creature, which one would you be?

A A mermaid or merman.

B A vampire.

C A werewolf.

D A centaur.

7. Which meal sounds best?

A Tofu, brown rice, green tea.

B Hamburger, French fries, soda.

C Roast chicken, mashed potatoes, milk.

D Lobster, scalloped potatoes, sparkling water.

Survival expert? Or lost without luxuries? Turn to page 141 to add up your score and find out how long you would survive!

10 INSTRUMENTS FROM THE VEGETABLE ORCHESTRA OF VIENNA, AUSTRIA

1. Pumpkin drum (with carrot drumsticks)
2. Celery guitar
3. Carrot recorder
4. Eggplant clapper
5. Celeriac bongo
6. Pepper horn
7. Leek violin
8. Rhubarb twanger
9. Radish bass flute
10. Parsley shaker

8 MUSICIANS WHO HAVE APPEARED ON *THE SIMPSONS* AS THEMSELVES

1. Britney Spears
2. Justin Bieber
3. Katy Perry
4. Lady Gaga
5. Chris Martin of Coldplay
6. 50 Cent
7. Elton John
8. Dolly Parton

TOP 20

bestselling artists of ALL TIME

1. The Beatles
2. Elvis Presley
3. Michael Jackson
4. Madonna
5. Elton John
6. Led Zeppelin
7. Pink Floyd
8. Mariah Carey
9. Celine Dion
10. Whitney Houston
11. AC/DC
12. Queen
13. The Rolling Stones
14. ABBA
15. Eminem
16. Garth Brooks
17. The Eagles
18. Rihanna
19. U2
20. Billy Joel

7 INSANELY VALUABLE INSTRUMENTS

1. A violin made by Antonio Stradivari in 1721, known as "Lady Blunt," sold for $2.1 million in 2011.

2. The piano that John Lennon composed the song "Imagine" on sold for $2.08 million.

3. Eric Clapton's "Blackie" Stratocaster guitar sold for $959,500.

4. A 5-piece drum kit used by the Who's Keith Moon sold for $252,487.

5. Jazz player Charlie Parker's Grafton saxophone sold for over $146,000.

6. A drumstick that belonged to Led Zeppelin's John Bonham sold for $63,000!

7. Jazz musician Dizzy Gillespie's trumpet sold for $55,000.

9 toy facts that are more than child's play

1. A Slinky **is made of 63 feet of wire.**

2. Kermit the Frog **is left-handed.**

3. Mr. Potato Head **was the first toy advertised on TV.**

4. The LEGO Group **is the world's biggest manufacturer of tires. It produces 318 million tiny tires every year!**

5. Play-Doh **was originally used to clean wallpaper. The recipe is a secret.**

6. Silly Putty **went to the moon on** *Apollo 8*. **The astronauts used it to stabilize their tools.**

7. 5 billion **Monopoly houses have been made since 1935.**

8. The record **for playing Monopoly underwater is 1,080 hours.**

9. The yo-yo **is one of the oldest toys in the world. It was once used as a weapon.**

6 deep, dark secrets about Barbie

1. **Barbie's full name** is Barbara Millicent Roberts.

2. **Barbie traveled to space** in 1965, 4 years before a human walked on the Moon.

3. **Barbie's birthday** is March 9, 1959.

4. **Barbie's first pet** was a horse named Dancer.

5. **Barbie has had** over 150 jobs.

6. **One Barbie** is sold every 3 seconds.

Darth Vader

Kermit the Frog

1. LEGO toys
2. Monopoly
3. Dungeons & Dragons
4. Wii
5. Nintendo Entertainment System (NES)

6. PlayStation
7. Scrabble
8. Scalextric cars
9. Trivial Pursuit
10. Game Boy

4 toys you could buy if you saved your allowance FOREVER

1. A prototype of G.I. Joe **made in 1963 sold for $200,000.**

2. A Steiff teddy bear **named Teddy Girl sold for $171,600.**

3. The original Barbie **recently sold for $27,450.**

4. A Darth Vader action figure **(from 1978, with a double-telescoping lightsaber) sold for $7,000.**

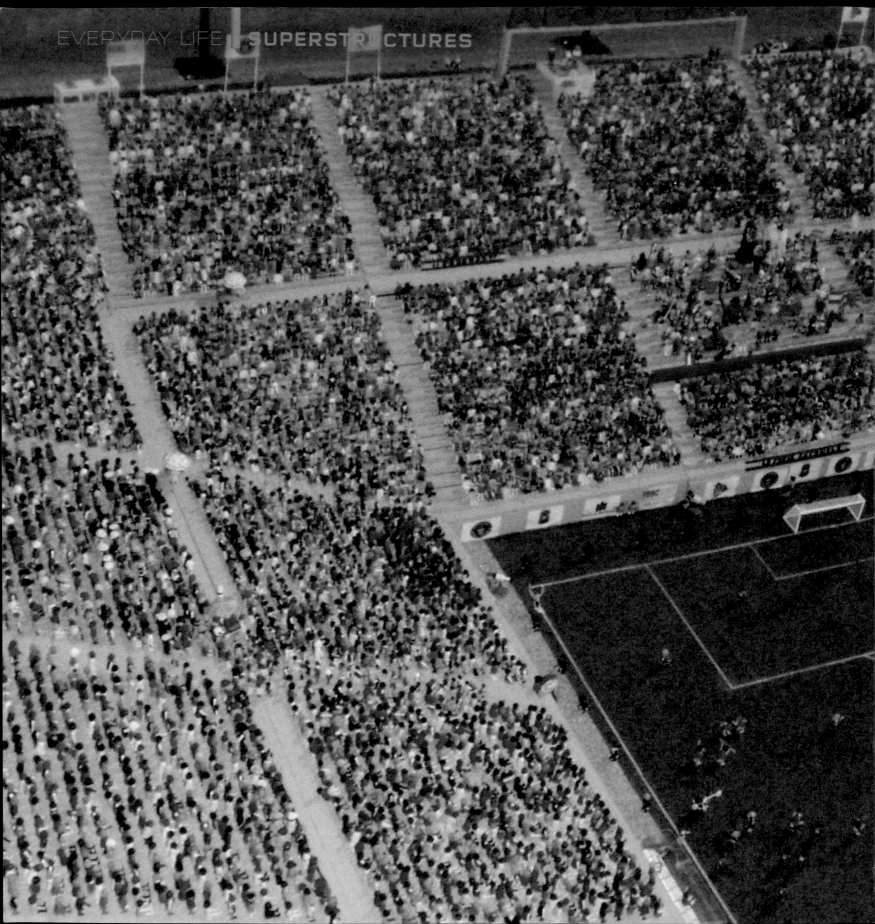

4 epic toy **super-**structures

1. LEGO model
The largest LEGO structure ever built was a Star Wars X-wing. It took 32 LEGO masters and over 5 million pieces to build it. It could fit a human.

2. Marble run
The longest measured 4,221 feet. It took 9 students a month to build it, and it took 10 minutes for a marble to complete the run.

3. Domino topple
The world record was broken in 2008. 89 people from 13 countries spent 8 weeks setting up 4.3 million dominoes. See it on YouTube!

4. Playmobil display
The largest Playmobil display is in Spain. It consists of 68,808 figurines, and it includes a busy city, a medieval battle, and a packed soccer stadium.

Answers

SCORING: Give yourself 1, 2, 3, or 4 points for each answer, based on the keys below. Then add up your points for each quiz to find out your results!

What ENDANGERED ANIMAL are you?

SCORING:

1. A=3; B=1; C=2; D=4

2. A=4; B=3; C=1; D=2

3. A=1; B=3; C=2; D=4

4. A=3; B=2; C=4; D=1

5. A=3; B=4; C=1; D=2

6. A=1; B=3; C=4; D=2

7. A=4; B=1; C=2; D=3

YOUR SCORE:

7–10: Monarch butterfly. Flap your orange, black, and cream wings. Your beautiful colors warn predators that you taste terrible.

11–14: Macaw. You're a colorful character! This big, brightly colored bird comes from South America. Some macaws can even talk!

15–17: Chimpanzee. Go bananas! Chimps are among our closest relatives. They are endangered partly because their habitat is shrinking.

18–20: Giant panda. Pandemonium! You're the cutest endangered animal in the world. You eat bamboo, you live in China, and you are adorable.

21–24: Elephant. Never forget! Elephants are found in both Africa and Asia. Both types are endangered.

25–28: Tiger. You've earned your stripes! You're the biggest big cat in the world. Everyone admires your beautiful orange-and-black coloring—and fears your ferocious teeth.

What PREHISTORIC BEAST are you?

SCORING:

1. A=4; B=1; C=3; D=2

2. A=2; B=4; C=3; D=1

3. A=3; B=2; C=4; D=1

4. A=1; B=4; C=3; D=2

5. A=4; B=3; C=1; D=2

6. A=2; B=4; C=3; D=1

7. A=4; B=3; C=1; D=2

YOUR SCORE:

7–10: Woolly mammoth. Scientists may someday be able to clone this enormous fuzzball. Good news or bad news? Either way, it's BIG news.

11–14: Three-toed sloth. Slow and sluggish, this big sloth was related to modern sloths—and it was just as poky.

15–17: *Plesiosaurus.* Flipping through the water, *Plesiosaurus* looked like a sea monster. And at up to 50 feet long, it was big enough to be truly monstrous!

18–20: Pterodactyl. Soaring over the prehistoric landscape, scavenging for dead animals and other tasty morsels, this giant flying reptile cast a shadow over the land.

21–24: Saber-toothed tiger. With sleek, striped fur and long, pointy teeth, this relative of today's big cats was fearsome and ferocious. Bad kitty!

25–28: *Tyrannosaurus rex.* This meat-eating giant stomped across the land, eating every creature that got in its way. *Rawr!* Too bad about the teensy little arms.

What VOLCANIC ERUPTION are you?

SCORING:

1. A=1; B=2; C=3; D=4
2. A=1; B=3; C=2; D=4
3. A=3; B=2; C=4; D=1
4. A=4; B=2; C=3; D=1
5. A=1; B=4; C=3; D=2
6. A=4; B=3; C=2; D=1
7. A=4; B=2; C=1; D=3

YOUR SCORE:

7–10: Kilauea. You're the most active volcano on Earth! Your very name means "spewing" in Hawaiian. But you don't spew way up into the air . . . your lava flows slowly across the land. Get out of the way!

11–14: Eyjafjallajökull. In 2010, Iceland's Eyjafjallajökull erupted—and created a massive cloud of ash and dust that grounded most of the planes in Europe. More than 10 million travelers were affected!

15–17: Mount Vesuvius. You're the most famous volcanic explosion in history! When Italy's Vesuvius erupted in 79 CE, it buried the town of Pompeii under volcanic ash—preserving it for thousands of years.

18–20: Mount Pelée. When Martinique's Mount Pelée erupted in 1902, it killed almost every person on the island. One of the few survivors was being held in solitary confinement in a basement jail cell.

21–24: Krakatau. You're the second-biggest eruption in recorded history! Krakatau's eruption in 1883 killed more than 30,000 people in Indonesia, and its name is still known and feared today.

25–28: Mount Tambora. You're the biggest, deadliest eruption in recorded history! Tambora rocked Indonesia in 1815, eventually causing a volcanic winter that spread across the globe and changed the course of history.

What ELEMENT of the PERIODIC TABLE are you?

SCORING:

1. A=1; B=2; C=3; D=4
2. A=1; B=3; C=2; D=4
3. A=4; B=3; C=2; D=1
4. A=4; B=3; C=2; D=1
5. A=2; B=3; C=4; D=1
6. A=3; B=2; C=1; D=4
7. A=3; B=4; C=2; D=1

YOUR SCORE:

7–10: Sometimes you seem to be everywhere at once! You are hydrogen, atomic number 1.

11–14: Handy and helpful, you are carbon, atomic number 6.

15–17: Bright and noble, you are neon, atomic number 10.

18–20: Strong and practical, you are iron, atomic number 26.

21–24: Beautiful and useful, you are gold, atomic number 79.

25–28: Full of energy and a little hot-tempered, you are uranium, atomic number 92.

What WORLD-CHANGING INVENTION are you?

SCORING:

1. A=1; B=2; C=4; D=3
2. A=1; B=3; C=2; D=4
3. A=2; B=1; C=3; D=4
4. A=1; B=3; C=4; D=2
5. A=4; B=3; C=2; D=1
6. A=4; B=2; C=3; D=1
7. A=3; B=2; C=1; D=4

YOUR SCORE:

7–10: The vacuum cleaner swept the nation.

11–14: Soap washed away the competition.

15–17: The sewing machine had people in stitches.

18–20: The automobile drove progress.

21–24: The telephone had everyone talking.

25–28: The wheel kept things rolling.

What FAMOUS SCIENTIST are you?

SCORING:

1. A=3; B=1; C=2; D=4
2. A=2; B=3; C=1; D=4
3. A=3; B=4; C=1; D=2
4. A=1; B=3; C=2; D=4
5. A=3; B=2; C=1; D=4
6. A=4; B=2; C=3; D=1
7. A=3; B=4; C=1; D=2

YOUR SCORE:

7–10: Jonas Salk. Salk's invention, a vaccine that protects children and adults from polio, has saved countless lives. He donated the vaccine to the world, with no thought of personal profit. "There is no patent," he said. "Could you patent the Sun?" Like Salk, you are brilliant and caring!

11–14: Neil deGrasse Tyson. Tyson, an astrophysicist, is also a great science communicator. He shares his knowledge with the world, in terms that everyone can understand. Like Tyson, you are brilliant and down-to-earth!

15–17: Marie Curie. A pioneer in the study of radioactivity, Curie discovered two elements, polonium and radium. Her work led to many lifesaving advances in medicine, including X-rays and radiology. Like Curie, you are brilliant and brave!

18–20: Galileo Galilei. The ultimate Renaissance man, Galileo was an astronomer, a physicist, a mathematician, and a philosopher. He was persecuted for his conviction that the Earth revolves around the Sun. Like Galileo, you are brilliant and inspiring!

21–24: Albert Einstein. Einstein, the greatest scientist of the 20th century, developed a theory of relativity that paved the way for an astonishing range of breakthroughs. Like Einstein, you are brilliant and innovative!

25–28: Nikola Tesla. The eccentric Tesla was a man of mystery and intrigue. And his work was years ahead of his time—he proposed wireless communication in 1893! Like Tesla, you are brilliant and creative!

Where should you LIVE?

SCORING:

1. A=1; B=4; C=2; D=3
2. A=2; B=3; C=4; D=1
3. A=2; B=1; C=3; D=4
4. A=1; B=4; C=2; D=3
5. A=3; B=2; C=4; D=1
6. A=1; B=3; C=2; D=4
7. A=2; B=3; C=1; D=4

YOUR SCORE:

7–10: On a farm, way out in the country. Farm living is the way to go for you! Move out to the country and enjoy peace and quiet.

11–14: Rolla, MO. This town, home to about 20,000 people, is surrounded by rolling green hills and beautiful natural scenery. For you, it's the best of both worlds!

15–17: San Diego, CA. Sunny Southern California! Beaches, a fantastic zoo, a bustling city—what more could you want?

18–20: Orlando, FL. Warm weather plus the world's greatest theme parks make this the place for you!

21–24: Tokyo, Japan. Exciting Tokyo always embraces the newest and hottest trends—just like you do!

25–28: New York City, NY. The hustling, bustling Big Apple! Can you make it there? Then you can make it anywhere! Go, go, go!

What JOB is right for you?

SCORING:

1. A=4; B=1; C=3; D=2
2. A=2; B=3; C=4; D=1
3. A=1; B=4; C=2; D=3
4. A=4; B=3; C=1; D=2
5. A=1; B=3; C=2; D=4
6. A=3; B=4; C=2; D=1
7. A=3; B=2; C=1; D=4

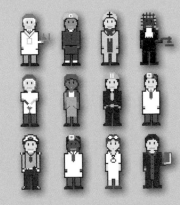

YOUR SCORE:

7–10: You're responsible and caring, and you're willing to work hard to achieve your goals. You should be a dentist.

11–14: You ask the big questions, and you want to fight for justice. You should be a lawyer.

15–17: You want to share ideas and knowledge with people everywhere. You should be a teacher or a librarian.

18–20: You want to help people get healthy and stay healthy, and you're up for a challenge. You should be a doctor or a nurse.

21–24: You enjoy helping people and protecting them— and you also love excitement! You should be a firefighter or a police officer.

25–28: You love the spotlight! You should be an actor, a singer, or a dancer—definitely a performer!

How long would you SURVIVE?

SCORING:

1. A=4; B=3; C=1; D=2
2. A=1; B=3; C=2; D=4
3. A=3; B=4; C=1; D=2
4. A=3; B=4; C=2; D=1
5. A=1; B=3; C=4; D=2
6. A=1; B=3; C=4; D=2
7. A=4; B=1; C=3; D=2

YOUR SCORE:

7–10: Maybe an hour? You won't make it too long without your screens, comfy bed, and tasty food.

11–14: 1 or 2 days, tops. No decent restaurants? This doesn't look good. Depends on if Mom makes it through, too.

15–17: 3 days to a week. You're pretty low maintenance. How long till the power comes back on?

18–20: 1 to 2 weeks. You'll eat whatever, and you're confident about your basic survival skills. But will that be enough?

21–24: 2 weeks to 6 months. You've got mad skills, and you're not afraid to use them to fight predators, build temporary shelter, and invent amusing new games.

25–28: 6 months to however long it takes. You got this.

Index

A

airplanes 106
amphibians (frogs, toads, salamanders, axolotls) 10, 19, 22, 33, 37, 48, 60
animal astronauts 60
animal babies 17
animal heroes 17, 60
animal senses 18-19
animal sounds 11, 17, 22-23
animals, deadly 22-23, 28, 35, 36
animals, endangered 33
animals, farmed 40, 64, 77, 102
animals, fastest 10-11, 29, 37
animals, largest 17, 29, 31, 35, 37
animals, loudest 17, 22-23, 35
animals on flags 117
animals, stinkiest 23, 37, 39
animals, strongest 39
animals, undersea 9, 10-11, 12, 16, 18, 19, 22, 23, 24, 25, 31, 33, 34-35, 44
answers 138-141
asteroid 62
astronauts 52, 54, 60, 58, 61, 66, 119
astronomy 52-53, 54-55
athletes 10-11

B

bacteria 13, 23
balls 48, 123, 124-125

beaches 34-35
birds 10, 11, 16, 17, 19, 22, 23, 25, 32, 33, 37, 64, 92, 111, 117
biting 10
blood 12, 13, 18, 19, 29, 49, 65, 90
brains 12, 93
breathing 35, 90
bridges 81, 117, 121
bugs *see* insects *and* spiders
buildings 80-81, 120, 137

C

cells 84
cities 44, 119, 120-121
climbing 112, 114, 122
coal tar 99
cold 47, 80, 119
colors 37, 49, 68, 69, 79
computers 79, 86-87
crops 77
crustaceans (shrimp, crabs, tongue worms) 11, 12, 23, 34
cyborgs 78-79

D

death 22-23, 28, 36, 40, 62-63, 66
deserts 45
darkness 62, 119
dinosaurs 28-29, 31, 119
direction finding 9, 18, 19, 39, 79
disasters 47, 62-63, 79, 81
discoveries 25, 44, 52, 67
diseases 12, 13, 64, 97
dominoes 137

E

Earth 44-45, 61, 62-63, 84
earthquakes 45, 79, 120
eating 10, 12, 92
ecology 45
eggs (insect) 12, 13
eggs (reptile) 29
electricity 9, 19
elements 36, 56-57, 64, 68-69, 92-93, 106
endangered species 14-15, 32-33
experiments 64-65
exploration 112-113, 114
explosions 41
extinction 32-33, 96-97
eyes 8-9, 19, 41, 64, 76, 79, 90, 93

F

farming 77
fire 19, 44, 45, 68
fish 8, 9, 10-11, 19, 22, 31, 33, 34, 35, 48
flight 11, 74, 114, 122
food 36, 98-99, 102-103, 104-105, 110
forces 64, 66-67
fruit 49, 102, 103
fuel 75
fungi 12

G

galaxies 52, 62
glass 80
gravity 64, 67
growth 11, 39, 90

H

hair 17, 19, 23, 24, 34, 93, 99
hearing 18, 19, 76, 79

I

heat 47, 49, 119
houses 80, 81
human body 78-79, 84, 90-91

infections 12, 13
insects 9, 10, 11, 12, 13, 18, 19, 20-21, 22, 23, 24, 31, 32, 34, 36, 37, 38-39, 84
intestines 12, 13
inventions 24, 58-59, 70-71, 72-73
islands 44

J

jewels 107
jumping 17, 39, 55, 114

K

kings 92

L

languages 96-97
LEGO 80, 134, 135, 136-137
light 39, 67, 85
lightning 45, 46, 47, 70

M

magnetism 19
math 84-85
medicines 77, 346, 37
meteorites 44, 53
money 84, 86, 106-107
mollusks (snails, clams, squid, octupuses) 10, 25, 34, 35
Moon 52, 54-55, 58, 67, 75
mountains 44, 52, 80, 113, 120
movies 77, 86, 97, 106, 126-127, 128-129
music 69, 132-133

N

names 24, 29, 97
night 19
numbers 84-85

O

oceans 10-11, 36, 67, 85
optical illusions 94-95

P

pain 19, 20-21, 40
parasites 12-13
periodic table 56-57, 68-69
pets 16-17, 60, 127
phobias 25
planets 54, 59, 60, 67, 74
plants 11, 37, 40-41
plants, dangerous 40-41
plants, fastest growing 11
plants, largest 37, 41
plants, oldest 41
Playmobil 137
poison 10, 19, 22-23, 40, 64, 68, 69, 99, 110
pollination 77
populations 84, 119, 121
predators 9, 11, 18, 19
prehistory 26-27, 28-29, 30-31, 32

Q

quizzes 14-15, 26-27, 42-43, 56-57, 72-73, 82-83, 100-101, 108-109, 130-131

R

radiation 62, 64
rain 119
rainforests 36-37, 44, 80, 120
reptiles (snakes, crocodiles, tortoises, lizards) 11, 18, 19, 24, 25, 28-29, 31, 33, 48, 49, 106

rivers 36
robots 76-77
running 10-11, 76

S

scent 18, 37, 39, 40, 41, 90, 106
scientists 64, 65, 67
senses 8-9, 18-19
sharks 11, 18-19, 22, 24, 30, 31, 33, 35, 46
sight 8-9, 18, 19, 25, 64
smell see scent
snakes 11, 18, 31, 32
solar system 52-53, 54-55, 67
soldiers 77, 79
sound 11, 85
space 44, 45, 52-53, 54-55, 58-59, 60-61, 62-63, 66, 67, 74, 77, 112, 117, 119, 134
speed 10-11, 52, 74, 75, 85, 125
spiders 9, 24, 37, 39, 49
sports 77, 122-123, 124-125
stars 52-53, 59, 62, 84
states 116-117
superheroes 128-129
survival 17, 36, 114-115
swimming 10-11, 114

T

taste 18, 19, 90
teeth 29, 34, 41, 91, 93
telescopes 52-53, 71
temperature 47, 85, 119
toys 80, 107, 134-135, 136-137

travel 59, 67, 70, 74-75, 112-113, 120-121, 134
trees 36, 37, 40, 41, 80, 117

U

urine 54, 61, 91, 99, 110

V

vehicles 74-75
venom see poison
vibrations 19
viruses 87
vision see sight
volcanoes 42-43, 44, 45, 114, 120, 122

W X Y Z

walking 76, 90, 114
wars 17, 65, 69, 91, 102
weapons 68, 69, 87, 134
weather 19, 46-47, 48-49, 70, 81, 114, 118, 119, 121
whales 11, 23, 24, 31, 35
World War I 69
World War II 17, 65
work 108-109, 110-111
worms 12, 13, 34, 48, 110

Image credits